SAY YES TO
PROJECT
SUCCESS

SAY YES TO PROJECT SUCCESS

WINNING THE PROJECT MANAGEMENT GAME

KARTHIK RAMAMURTHY
SRIPRIYA NARAYANASAMY

Notion Press

Old No. 38, New No. 6
McNichols Road, Chetpet
Chennai - 600 031

First Published by Notion Press 2017
Copyright © Karthik Ramamurthy & Sripriya Narayanasamy 2017
All Rights Reserved.

ISBN 978-1-947949-03-4

Dedication

To the millions of project managers all over the world who boldly strive for project success while battling complex scope, compressed timelines, tight budgets, demanding customers, and limited resources.

We face the same challenges. We feel the same pain.

We are with you.

Contents

Appendices

Ten Golden Keys to Project Success

From Padma Vibhushan Dr E Sreedharan, the "Metro Man"

1. In projects, "time is money." Time overruns will certainly lead to cost overruns. Punctuality should, therefore, be the cornerstone of management's work culture. Reverse countdown clocks can be a useful tool towards this.

2. Integrity is indispensable at every level, particularly with top management. Integrity does not mean just honesty or absence of corruption. It also means practicing "high moral values."

3. Professional competence is the backbone of success. If in-house expertise is not available, you should not hesitate to borrow expertise or engage qualified experts.

4. The project team has to be slim and efficient, avoiding unproductive layers.

5. Speedy decision-making is critical. Avoiding multiple decision-making layers is helpful in taking quick decisions.

6. Project leaders should be a role model to the rest of the team. They should inspire confidence, trust, and respect. They should take proactive steps to keep the team motivated.

7. Project planning and execution should cause least inconvenience or dislocation to the community or the public.

8. Respect "Mother Nature" and accord top priority to the protection of the environment.

9. Treat vendors and contractors as valued stakeholders.

10. Goodwill of the client should be accorded more importance than profits.

Dr. E Sreedharan is a true legend in project management. He was named in *TIME* magazine's Asia's Heroes list in 2003 and received India's second highest civilian honor, the "Padma Vibhushan" in 2008. Dr. Sreedharan is credited with changing the face of public transport in India with his leadership in building the incredibly complex and challenging Konkan Railway and the Delhi Metro projects. Besides adding significant value as an advisor for several other Metro projects in India, he served on the United Nations' High-Level Advisory Group on Sustainable Transport.

An amazingly simple and humble man, he values integrity, hard work and commitment, professional excellence, and commitment to society.

Acknowledgments

Nandri, Kritagyataa. These words mean "gratitude" in the ancient Indian languages, Tamizh and Sanskrit.

Writing a book was a daunting project. We would never have made it but for many people who were generous with their knowledge, ideas, time, and talent.

Publishing experts advise authors to keep the acknowledgments section short and limit the number of people thanked. We respectfully disagree.

First, our parents.

We are immensely grateful to Kamala Ramamurthy, an amazingly strong and resourceful lady, entrepreneur, and social worker, for encouraging us to think big and always nudging us to get the job done. We had planned on 26 cartoons and 52 experts. She challenged us to do double.

We are deeply indebted to V Ramamurthy, who retired from the prestigious Indian Administrative Service, the civil service that runs the Indian government. He is a man of so many talents that it is tough to list them all: author, poet, television personality, quiz master, cryptic crossword compiler, sports broadcaster, dance and music critic, and so on. He helped us in many ways: Conceptualizing, providing plot ideas, and editing. His biggest contribution? He challenged us to cut 30% of the words from early drafts and to use simple, clear, and concise language.

We heartfully thank R Jayalakshmi and P V Narayanasamy, both accomplished teachers, for constant motivation and moral support. They kept tabs on our progress every day, which kept us on track.

Rahul, our amazingly multi-talented teenage son, international spelling bee champion, cricketer, and voracious reader, played a key role in this book. He turned out to be our biggest critic and constantly questioned us on plots and concepts. We dreaded his answers to the question, "on a scale of one to ten, what grade would you give this chapter?" When the grades weren't above eight, we were forced to rewrite to get better marks! Special thanks to him.

We feel a deep sense of gratitude to Padma Vibhushan Dr. E Sreedharan, legendary project management guru. We are honored that he created time, to give us his precious "Ten Golden Keys to Project Success," which begins this book.

Our special thanks go to Brajesh Kaimal, entrepreneur and project management expert, who generously arranged for us to meet Dr. E Sreedharan.

We are very grateful to K Srinivasamurthy, owner of KK Books and Director of Quality & Productivity Publishing. He gave us regular doses of encouragement for two years. His invaluable advice, based on decades of publishing experience, added real value.

We owe special thanks to Raj Kalady, Managing Director, Project Management Institute (PMI) India, Prasannaa Sampathkumar and Koushik Srinivasan, Conference Chair and

Director respectively, for the opportunity to release our book at the prestigious PMI India National Conference 2017.

We thank Sivaram Athmakuri, project management expert, consultant, and trainer, for the fantastic value-adding ideas, manuscript review, and adding the agile flavor to many Chapters of the book. Ramam Atmakuri and Tejas Sura, long-time PMI volunteer leaders and our mentors, were generous with valuable suggestions on the storylines in many sections.

Our book includes project management insights from over 2000 projects in 119 countries and 54 industry segments. Over a 100 global PM gurus contributed valuable perspectives on delivering project success. Many of them are authors in their own right and were given the tough task of limiting their insights to 120 words. We are indebted to them for sharing their wealth of expertise with the project management community.

We are extremely thankful to Sasi Kumar, Dr. Chakradhar Iyyunni, Ilango Vasudevan, Zahara Khan, Deepa Bhide, and John Watson, all project management experts. They gave us the precious gift of their time, adding significant value by carefully reviewing our manuscripts for validity, accuracy, and readability. Our deep gratitude goes to veteran photographer Krishnan Desikan and his son Shantanu. They exemplified passion, perfection, and professionalism in clicking our profile pictures for our book's back cover.

We were lucky to have an awesome "Double A" team of talented cartoonists, Amber Marfatia and Arun Ramkumar, who competed to pitch ideas for cartoons. It was healthy competition, which resulted in brilliant toons that add a light touch to the serious topic of project management. Throughout the book, Amber's cartoons are drawn in square shapes while Arun's toons are presented in rectangular form.

We thank Venkatesh Krishnamoorthy, our book's copy editor who went beyond his brief of just checking grammar and style. He added tangible value with suggestions on structuring story lines and Chapter design, in addition to boosting our confidence levels on many instances.

We thank the entire team at Notion Press. Our publishers were professional and helpful throughout. Naveen Valsakumar gave us the confidence that our dream was achievable. Vandana was generous with excellent marketing ideas. L Karthikeyan and G Thaatcher added value through their helpful yet professional project management contributions. H Vairamuthu gave excellent inner page design options and did a terrific job with the typesetting. We are also very thankful to the several other amazing Notion Press team members who contributed to the cover design and social media marketing.

Arigato, Dhanyavaad, Danke, Gracias, Faldies, Kop Khun, Kiitos, Kritagyataa, Mahalo, Merci, Nandri, Ngiabonga, Paldies, Shukran, Terima Kasih, Thank you!

Karthik Ramamurthy
Sripriya Narayanasamy

Introduction

Projects fail. Frequently. Across industries. All over the world.

Project failures can be as high as a frightening 70% as confirmed by several global surveys, including the "Chaos Reports" by the Standish Group.

We failed too. As developers, designers, and team leads who showed the most initiative and dynamism, we were pitchforked into project management with no training. It was like being blindfolded and left alone in a dangerous jungle.

We made mistakes. Many of them. We've shared a few of them in our book.

We've had bad bosses, terrible bosses. We've learned much from them: How not to demotivate people and crush their spirit. How not to be biased, unfair, or unethical.

We reported to some amazing leaders. They were so amazing that good leaders who came later paled in comparison. We've learned from them all.

Around 15 years ago, we had our first formal training in this area. We learned the theory of project management, earned a prestigious international certification, and started applying the principles to our projects.

At first, it wasn't easy. We continued to fail. We learned from those failures.

With sustained effort and continual learning, we started succeeding. Small successes first, baby steps. We learned a lot from amazing mentors and colleagues with more experience and successes than ours. Our project success rates grew.

With a preschooler son, we realized that working 12 to 14 hours a day for someone else was not a palatable option.

Taking a leap of faith, we founded KeyResultz, a firm that would help companies leverage best practices in global project management to boost project success.

To keep our knowledge and skills up-to-date, we joined the local PMI Chapter. Soon, we were volunteering and then training professionals through certification preparation courses. Sharing our best practices with participants from many industries, we learned about the most common challenges they faced in projects.

Participants would often ask us to recommend books focused on practical application of best practices. We found many great books that covered tools and techniques in project management. However, we didn't find too many dedicated to practical tools and techniques to deliver successful projects.

The theory is essential to understanding project management. But practical tools and techniques are what will get you real results. A famous Tamil adage says, "Don't cook eggplant dishes with printed pictures of the vegetable." Theory is great, but practice brings results!

Amidst widespread failure, those who deliver results are likely to ride the fast elevator to career success. There are many shining examples. Padma Vibhushan Dr. E Sreedharan, hailing from a small village, started as an engineer. Over time, he grew to become one of the most accomplished project managers in the world. Similarly, A M Naik, Chairman of Larsen & Toubro (L&T), one of India's most respected conglomerates, also had humble beginnings. He started at L&T as a junior engineer.

What were the key ingredients in their success stories? Determination. Hard work. Continuous learning. A fourth recurring theme was a consistent track record of delivering project success.

Over the past decade, we put together a set of tips and techniques that helped us to deliver many successful projects across four continents. Clients we helped suggested their tweaks to our approach. Later, they shared personal success stories in implementing the techniques.

Thus was born the idea of our book.

In researching material for this book, we carried out an in-depth analysis of project failure across 50+ global studies. We found many recurring themes which are listed in Appendix A.

To increase the breadth and depth of knowledge and experience, we invited 100+ experts with experience in delivering project success across 2,000+ projects in 119 countries and 54 industry segments. A full list of contributors is available in Annexure B. Lists of countries and industry sectors covered are provided in Annexures C and D respectively.

This book, therefore, gives you a collection of practical, field-tested techniques to help you achieve project success!

How do you use this book?

We have tried very hard to make this book as easy to use as possible:

- As project managers, we lead busy lives. We don't always have the time to read a book from cover to cover. We, therefore, structured the book to include 52 chapters, each typically just three pages long.

- Each chapter is standalone and deals with a unique topic. You can pick any one and learn a tip, technique or principle valuable for project success.

- Storytelling, using the compelling Situation–Impact–Resolution format, conveys the tip, technique, or principle.

- Two global experts who share their insights in their particular area of project management expertise augment the storyline.

- Don't have time to read the entire story? Every chapter ends with a "Keys to Success" section, which summarizes the material in the chapter. Where relevant, a bullet point discusses how the tip or technique in the chapter applies to agile projects.

- How do you choose chapters to read? Start with your biggest current project management problem. Appendix A connects the top project failure factors with specific chapters in the book that provide possible solutions.

This book is a valuable resource in helping you deliver project success. We look forward to hearing your own success stories through our website, projectsuccessbook.com.

The website is a treasure trove of expert blogs, crowd-sourced success tips and a detailed glossary of terms in this book.

You can also email us your success stories and feedback to projectsuccess@keyresultz. com. We may feature your success stories on the website.

We can help your organization with result oriented consulting and project success workshops based on the techniques in this book. Details are available in Appendix G. Appendix H contains a short glossary of the technical project management terms most used in this book.

Happy reading! We wish you successful projects!

Me, CEO?

"Wow, what a start to the day," Ganesh told himself. He had been handpicked to lead a prestigious project. Project success would bring him that long-awaited promotion.

The new project that his company had won against stiff competition involved developing an innovative e-security solution for a global pharmaceutical company. The scope was challenging, and timelines compressed. With smart leadership and diligence, however, the project was certainly doable.

Ganesh's euphoria was short-lived. He was unnerved by some parts of the contract his boss had just shared. Page 87 specified stiff penalties that could nullify all projected profits. More shocking was the cancellation clause on page 93. It was applicable if deliverables didn't meet critical acceptance criteria.

Project failure was just not an option for Ganesh.

He had recently attended a "Project Success" workshop. One of the key principles he learned was the importance of the project manager playing the role of the project CEO. Ganesh read the relevant section of the workshop handout:

- Understand the big picture of client priorities.
- Develop a simple yet strong vision statement to achieve those benefits.
- Distill the project's vision into an aspirational project slogan and, if possible, a simple logo.
- Communicate the vision passionately to the entire team. The project manager's passion and energy have a tangible effect that rubs off onto team members.
- Start communicating early, right from project kick-off.
- Reinforce the message at regular intervals.

The next day, Ganesh discussed his vision with his three module leaders. They finalized the internal project name, "Fortress," with the slogan, "Safe as a Fort!" The quartet ideated a logo with an ancient fort but did not have the graphic design skills to develop a logo.

They asked Thomas, the team's most talented designer, for help. Excited, Tom showed them a simple logo he had designed for a previous project named "A-Star," short for Assessment, Standardization, and Refinement. The project slogan was "A* or nothing!"

Impressed, the team asked Tom to design a simple logo. By 6 p.m., the team had this elegant logo. Ganesh requested the design to be included in all internal project communications.

SAFE AS A FORT!

At project kick-off, Ganesh passionately communicated the key benefits the project would bring to the firm. Tackling the "What's In It For Me" question, he assured them that project success would bring personal career growth for everyone.

" Oh that manager is a CEO - 'Can-Do Energy Officer'!

"Like the fort in our logo, let's hold strongly together. Let's defend our company's name. Let's build stronger forts in the future. With this talented team, I'm 100% sure that we will!"

The motivated team confidently charged forward, conquering one milestone after another. Tough challenges were overcome, with everyone pitching in to help. Ganesh was always ready with strong, supportive leadership to troubleshoot issues the team couldn't handle.

The product was delivered a few days ahead of schedule. The customer was delighted.

As the team celebrated, they were told that an even tougher project was waiting for them. "Bring it on," they chorused!

EXPERT INSIGHTS

Rick A. Morris PMP, CSAM

Owner of R2 Consulting, LLC.

Projects in England, Germany, Italy, USA. **Industries:** Banking, Entertainment, Finance, Government, Information Technology, Insurance, Manufacturing, Medical Devices, Nonprofit, Pharmaceutical, Retail, and many others.

Rick owns R2 Consulting, LLC. He is an evangelist for project management and an internationally sought after professional speaker who can be heard weekly on his live radio show "The Work/Life Balance."

When asked what they do for a living, many project managers fumble with a long and technical explanation when there is a much simpler response: Project managers make dreams come true.

When you need a new product, building, task, thought, idea, or first to market strategy, there may be many domain experts at the organization. However, a project manager is best equipped to ensure the highest quality and productivity from that team. If the process and training of a project manager are trusted, it will enable the value, which allows the greatest innovations and rewards to follow.

A Chandrasekaran PMP, PMI-ACP, CSM, CSP, CRISC, ITIL (F), SAFe Agilist

Founder Director, Infocareer Pvt. Ltd.

Projects in Cambodia, India, Japan, Malaysia, Myanmar, Singapore, UK, USA. **Industries:** Education, Financial Services, Government, Information Technology, Manufacturing.

In 1999-2000, I was appointed Delivery Head (APAC) of an application software company in Singapore, leading a team of 300+. Within days, I received a cancellation notification on a prestigious government project, with threats of severe penalties.

In the crisis, I saw an opportunity. Temporarily stepping down as Delivery Head, I took on the role of the struggling project manager. Wearing the CEO hat, I communicated a big picture vision, challenging my team to achieve the impossible: Turn around the project and delight the customer. Acting fairly and openly, I regularly motivated my team.

The project was turned around in a matter of weeks. The customer started trusting us and gave us more revenue. Lesson learned? Think and act like a CEO, and you can achieve significant results!

KEYS TO SUCCESS

- Project managers have as much authority and power as they want as long as they are willing to be accountable for it.
- You have the ability to significantly increase chances of project success by being a dynamic, proactive, and motivational leader.
- Even if your project is small, you should think big.
- Start by thinking, acting, and communicating like the CEO of your project.
- Create a powerful yet simple vision statement. Where relevant, develop a catchy project name and simple logo to help your team rally around the goal.
- Communicate the vision of your project right from the early stages.
- Repeat the message at frequent intervals to ensure continuity.
- Be transparent, fair, and entirely ethical and encourage all team members to follow your lead. This builds trust, a critical requirement for project success.

02   Engaged to Succeed

"Has the Peter Principle[1] hit me? Have I reached the point where my weaknesses will hurt me?" Lost in thoughts, Gokul was feeling a little low.

He was ruminating on Aisha's sharpish words at the project's weekly meeting: "Gokul, we've yet to get the CEO's sign off on cost baselines. Our project stands stalled." It wasn't the first time the project was being delayed due to limited interaction with management.

Gokul was proud of his meteoric growth. Many in the firm envied him. Clarity of thought, diligence in planning, hard work, and flawless execution had seen him progress from a trainee to a project manager in just three years.

A man of few words, he preferred to let his work do the talking. Being an introvert, he did not engage with his bosses for small talk. This approach was now hurting his project. Gokul knew that he had to do something. Something fast!

Googling for "Sponsor Engagement" and "Project Management," he found a PMI Pulse of the Profession In-Depth® Report[2] on Executive Sponsor Engagement. The report stressed that actively engaged executive sponsors were a top driver of project success. Gokul searched further, and noted down distinct patterns:

a. Unclear linkage of project benefits to the business caused sponsor disinterest.

b. Management didn't have the time to spend with the project team.

c. When a project was stuck, there was no help forthcoming.

How could he tackle these problems? Gokul dug deeper, researching several blogs and articles. He jotted down these points:

a. Assess sponsor and organizational expectations. Find out what motivates them. Check whether some of your project's goals can help sponsors reach their objectives.

b. Talk the language of management. Project managers often use too much jargon which is not easily understood by others.

c. Obtain firm time commitments. Schedule regular meetings. Strike a balance between too much and too little. Don't overburden sponsors by copying them in all project-related e-mails. Invite them only to the most important meetings.

d. Communicate bad news on the project quickly and honestly. Let sponsors hear from you first, but don't go to them with problems alone. Instead, present plausible solutions.

Working on these insights, Gokul formulated a clear plan. Taking one sure-footed step at a time, he started implementing his plan.

First, he read company CEO Jonathan's latest speeches to understand the firm's vision and long-term strategy. He accessed YouTube videos of his CEO's recent interviews to business channels. He also learned that Jonathan had a passion for football.

---

[1] https://en.wikipedia.org/wiki/Peter_principle

[2] http://www.pmi.org/-/media/pmi/documents/public/pdf/learning/thought-leadership/pulse/executive-sponsor-engagement.pdf

The next day, Gokul scheduled a meeting with the CEO. He had developed a short presentation deck showing how his project's objectives aligned with the organization's goals.

At the meeting, he stressed on his project's benefits. He used football terms such as "overhead kicks," "sweeper keeper," and "brilliant saves" to describe project achievements. Impressed, Jonathan agreed to Gokul's request for a fortnightly one-hour meeting.

Every three months, Gokul invited the CEO to speak to his team. Highlights of these speeches were covered in the company's newsletter. Everyone in the organization knew by now that the project had the CEO's blessings. This impression opened many doors for the project.

As the project team celebrated the completion of a significant milestone, Gokul told Aisha: "Thanks a million, buddy! If you hadn't chided me to engage with management, we wouldn't be here today!"

EXPERT INSIGHTS

Thomas Walenta PMP, PgMP

Program and Project Management Consultant (Independent).

Projects in Austria, Czech Republic, France, Germany, India, Japan, Poland, Romania, Russia, Singapore, Slovakia, UAE, UK, USA. **Industries:** Automotive, Banking, Consumer Sales, Industrial Electronics, Information Technology, Insurance, Justice (ministry), Logistics, Utilities.

40+ years experience. Contributor to projects since 1974. Full-time cross-industry project manager since 1988. Served as PMI volunteer for close to 20 years now, in various roles such as Chapter President and Board Member. Awarded PMI Fellow in 2012.

A critical question to clarify in the beginning is how to proceed with top management involvement during the project: Ask who will be the project sponsor. Be sure to state what you need from the sponsor: at least a monthly informal meeting, a regular steering committee and support with representing the project to the organization, e.g., with resource acquisition, conflict resolution, embedding project outputs into the organization. Maybe the project requestor does not have sufficient time to support your project. In such a case, he may choose to assign the sponsor role to someone else.

Sumit Kumar Sinha M.Tech, PMP

General Manager, Ericsson India Global Services Pvt. Ltd.

Projects in India, Malaysia, Singapore, UAE, USA. **Industries:** Airlines, Banking, Information Technology, Telecommunications.

27+ years of rich expertise in delivery leadership, business development, design, information technology project management. President–PMI West Bengal Chapter.

Top management commitment is a key driver for project success. How can you enhance engagement?

Start by understanding high-level priorities and bandwidth availability. Secure buy-in from senior stakeholders. Make sure you openly and sincerely appreciate the value they add to the project.

Invest time in setting up the right governance structure and in developing a comprehensive communication management plan. Deploy mechanisms to ensure that stakeholder expectations are recorded, actioned and tracked. Regularly collect feedback. Analyze feedback to find gaps between expectations and delivery. Discuss improvement plans with senior stakeholders and provide them opportunities to present leadership insights to your team.

Do these things well, and your engagement will grow. So will chances of your project's success.

KEYS TO SUCCESS

- Adequate sponsor engagement will result in newer, bolder, and speedier decisions; appropriate allotment of contingency funds, protect critical resources, etc., and is hence a top project success factor.
- Proactive steps to engage sponsors are a must for project success.
  - ➤ Understand what the sponsor expects from your project.
  - ➤ Align your project with organizational strategy.
  - ➤ Talk the language of management.
  - ➤ Obtain time commitments for engagement. Engage at the right levels – neither too little nor too much.
  - ➤ Communicate bad news quickly and truthfully. However, don't rush to your sponsor with just problems. Make sure you suggest solutions to the problems.
- In agile projects, writing requirements as user stories helps product owners and teams to communicate in plain English without technical jargon.
- User stories also help you promote the free flow of communication and build rapport among all stakeholders.

Aim Right

Gokul was upbeat on how the past three months had gone by.

Engaging company CEO Jonathan in his project had helped him achieve a dramatic turnaround of sponsor engagement. His rapport with the top boss was now the envy of many in the company. Gokul had also used innovative techniques such as implementing the Fish philosophy and appreciation circles to drastically boost engagement levels within his team.

Sergei, a manager heading another important project, met Gokul and requested help. Sergei's project was suffering from low levels of engagement. Gokul began by asking Sergei, "Have you read our company's Annual Report? Have you listened to our CEO's recent interviews? Do you read management's quarterly email blasts?"

Sergei sighed, "Who has the time for all of that? All we do is fight fires all day!"

Gokul replied, "It's your lack of engagement that causes many of those fires. I'm warning you. Many more fires are on the way if you don't invest time to understand our company's strategic goals and in engaging your team!

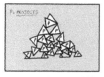
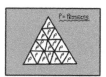

What a difference when everyone pulls together keeping in mind the bigger picture!

"The US and Europe are saturated. Jonathan wants us to explore Africa. The quarterly email last week emphasized the importance of improving profitability. What are you doing in these areas? Try connecting Marketing with your client's Durban subsidiary. Look at ways to cut unnecessary costs. These steps will show the boss that you're listening!"

Sergei now understood the seriousness of his issues. He resolved to work on them.

A week later, Manuela, Gokul's colleague and HR head, dropped him a note. She wanted to pick his brain on how he had drastically boosted his team's engagement levels.

Gokul, along with two team leads, attended a meeting with Manuela and her associates.

"We just finished analyzing results of the Employee Engagement Survey, which closed last week. Your team's numbers were crazy on the charts. We'd like to know what you guys have been doing differently."

Gokul said that apart from engaging the CEO, he had learned that an engaged team was critical to improved productivity. He had introduced the "Our Stars" program for instant appreciation. During team lunch on Thursday every week, two team members would address their colleagues for 15 minutes each on their areas of interest outside of work. These programs had been a roaring success, and the team was getting new inputs on more initiatives.

After gathering notes from the meeting with Gokul, the HR department launched company-wide weekly team get-togethers. They also implemented technology solutions for organization-wide experience sharing. The next half-yearly engagement survey results showed tangible improvements.

Gokul had achieved a two-way alignment. He realized two key things: his project was brought in line with company goals, and he helped the organization implement a best practice for team engagement. He wrote on his whiteboard: "Align. Communicate. Succeed. Grow!"

EXPERT INSIGHTS

C V Ramanatha Siva BBA, PGCBM, PMP, ITIL, CSM

Senior Development Manager, ITO Retail Digital Channels, Standard Chartered Bank, Singapore.

Projects in Ghana, Hong Kong, India, Indonesia, Kenya, Malaysia, Nigeria, Singapore, Tanzania, Thailand, UAE, Uganda, UK, USA, Zambia, Zimbabwe. **Industries:** Banking, FinTech, Information Technology, Manufacturing, Training.

21+ years of versatile global delivery and project management experience in the information technology services industry, primarily in digitization of banking and financial services. PMI volunteer and PMP since October 2007.

Urge team members to ask "what" and "why" rather than "how" (the nitty-gritty) before they commit to delivering projects. Those answers will help establish vital links between your project/program and organizational goals.

I've achieved significant success using four powerful techniques that grow team engagement, value delivery, and commitment to project success:

What's In It for Me?: *Helps connect personal aspirations with organizational goals.*

5 Whys: *Helps colleagues link project purpose to corporate objectives.*

Balcony & Dance Floor: *Most project teams operate at dance floor level, focusing on minor details. Taking the top-down balcony view helps connect to organizational strategy.*

Agile Approach (Kanban/Scrum): *Helps time box deliverables and build productive, self-organizing teams that collaborate to deliver real organizational value.*

Venkat Ramachandran MBA, PMP, ITIL, CSPO

Senior Product Owner, TD Bank Group, Canada.

Projects in Canada, India, Ireland, Philippines. **Industries:** Banking, Business Consulting, Healthcare, Information Technology, Insurance, Wealth Management.

25+ years of expertise in strategic planning, call center applications, e-business and content management applications, digital channels, business process re-engineering, project, program, account and vendor management. Volunteer experience: PMI Region Mentor, PMIef Engagement Committee, and President of PMI-CTT Chapter.

Many project teams enjoy functioning as renegade units charting their own courses. Innovation, independence, and individual creativity become convenient excuses to deviate from corporate roadmaps. However, projects not aligned to organizational strategy can severely suffer from the ill-effects of poor sponsor engagement.

It is critical for you as project manager to exhibit strong, proactive leadership. Talk to your team about the real benefits of your project aligning to organizational goals. Request senior company leaders to communicate to them on long-term strategy. Challenge team members to arrive at timeline and solution decisions that are in step with high-level strategy.

I introduced a group lunch or ice cream after every key milestone that demonstrated alignment. We recognized every team member for ideas on fitting the project jigsaw puzzle piece into the larger picture. As morale and motivation levels grew, productivity increased. We even delivered some products weeks earlier with zero severe defects!

KEYS TO SUCCESS

- Appropriate and timely sponsor engagement is a top factor in project success.
- Align project objectives to organizational goals to improve sponsor engagement.
- Start with understanding goals by reading through annual reports, media interviews, and internal email blasts.
- Work with your teams to find concrete steps that can increase alignment.
- Communicate points of alignment to sponsors.
- Actively look for ways to create two-way alignment. Work on scaling up best practices developed by your project team to the rest of the organization.
- In agile projects, every iteration begins with the product owner conveying what they want.
- At the end of every review, your team provides a demo of working software.
- This approach will ensure that your teams understand the critical needs of business and fulfill them with minimum effort.

04 Come on, Be Realistic!

Mike felt like he needed a long walk. The previous week, his boss Raghav had asked for a high-level time estimate on a complicated e-commerce project. Analyzing detailed requirements with his team, Mike had proposed a 13-month schedule, including a one-month buffer.

Raghav had sternly replied, "That's impossible. You need to complete in seven." Mike did not respond immediately. He told Raghav, "Let me talk to my team and get back to you on Tuesday."

Over the weekend, Mike's thoughts went back to a nightmare project two years ago. His team had estimated eight months with a 15% buffer. His previous boss had demanded that the project be completed in five. As an inexperienced project manager, Mike accepted the compressed timeline to please his boss.

Faced with an entirely impossible target, people just stop trying. Mike's team had sleep-walked through the project. They had pretended to work hard. Sincere efforts to motivate had failed. The project had finally taken 11 months to complete. Mike's company had lost the customer.

The furious boss had asked why the project took so long. Mike's answer was, "You and I both knew five months was never possible." The reply from the boss shocked Mike: "You accepted that timeline without complaint. We made promises to the customer based on your confidence!"

Mike was determined not to relive that nightmare.

Back at work on Monday, he called for a team meeting. He said, "Guys, we have a problem. Raghav is upset with 13 months. He wants seven. We know that's impossible. Let's rework our numbers and propose a new schedule."

The team revisited the original estimates. They looked at options such as doing work in parallel, automating tasks, and leveraging reusable code from company repositories. While retaining time buffers for critical and therefore risky tasks, they safely reduced a few other buffers.

The team now arrived at a 9.8-month project estimate. Adding a one-month buffer, Mike could now propose 11 months.

Mike wanted more: "What if the customer still insists on ten? We need a Plan B." Carlos, a project lead suggested that the team could ask for two more developers. Hasina, another lead, suggested that if they couldn't increase team size, three low-priority requirements could be moved to phase two.

Going back to Raghav, Mike gave details of how his team had smartly compressed the schedule. Making it clear that accepting a seven-month plan would be suicidal, he requested the boss to negotiate an 11-month deal.

Raghav appreciated Mike's approach.

Communicating the need for additional time, he told the client that he could accept the seven-month demand now and make them happy. But how would they feel when the promise was ultimately broken?

While the customer was unwilling to accept 11 months, they did relent for 10. Plan B was now in play.

Mike wrote of this experience in his project success blog. He titled it: "Underpromise. Overdeliver. Succeed!"

EXPERT INSIGHTS

Raghuram Sarangan B.E.

Former Vice President – Technology, Accenture Services India.

Projects in China, India, Philippines, Ireland, USA. **Industries:** Information Technology, Life Sciences, Professional Services.

20+ years of experience with 16+ in the information technology industry, including portfolio management of large programs with over 160+ people across five geographies.

Many project managers think setting realistic expectations means talking "only" with the client to understand their requirement and deadlines. But the key to success of a project is to set expectations to all stakeholders – most importantly your team and your boss.

Unless your team knows what is required, they cannot deliver. Hence project managers should not hide any information from their team: Be transparent. Be clear on what is expected by all other stakeholders from your team.

As for your client/boss, be clear on what your team can deliver. Do not give in to undue pressures. Neither overpromise to your client/boss nor underexpect from your team.

Olivier Lazar MSc., MBA, PfMP, PgMP, PMP, PMI-PBA, PMI-RMP, PMI-SP, ACP

COO and Managing Partner at the Valense Palatine Group.

Projects in Australia, Belgium, Canada, China, Egypt, France, Germany, India, Italy, Japan, Morocco, Netherlands, Poland, Russia, Saudi Arabia, Singapore, South Africa, Spain, Switzerland, Tunisia, Turkey, UAE, UK, Ukraine, USA. **Industries:** Several.

20+ years' experience in organizational architecture, portfolio management, organizational agility. 10+ years volunteering with PMI and PMIeF.

What is a realistic expectation? Is it something we can be 100% certain to achieve? Certainly not, since a project, by definition is something uncertain, implying a certain level of uncertainty.

What is uncertainty? It's a lack of quantitative information. Everything related to time, cost, effort, resources, etc. Everything requiring estimation. Estimation, which is also by definition uncertain. No estimation is 100% accurate. For if so, it's not an estimate anymore. It's a fact, it's a decision.

That level of accuracy in our estimates is, in fact, nothing else than a certain level of risk. If you want to have an estimate with 10% accuracy, it simply means you accept 20% of the risk on that estimate (± 10% around the average). Then uncertainty is risk. And risk is uncertainty.

From this statement, we can say that realistic means taking a proper account of risk. And not only threats, negative risk. But even more incorporating opportunities. Reversing the major threats you have identified, taking them as parameters of your project and exploiting the reversed opportunity.

This simple trick will allow you to establish a realistic target for your project, be it in terms of time, cost, or even scope.

KEYS TO SUCCESS

- Set realistic expectations from the start to steer your project in the right direction.
- When expectations are plenty, prioritization of the most important requirements will help you manage stakeholders better.
- Proactively explore alternative ways of meeting expectations. Useful techniques include value engineering, leveraging reusable code, requesting additional time, budget, or resources, and so on.
- If you believe that an expectation is impossible to meet, communicate the fact to the stakeholders at the earliest.
- Don't be afraid to say "No." Doing so requires courage and excellent communication skills. However, if you don't, say "No," you will be saying "Yes" to project failure!
- In agile projects, your team has the authority to determine the number of user stories they want to complete in an iteration. Product owners have the power to prioritize.
- Using this approach, you can promote transparency and encourage realistic expectation setting.

Must-Have Mentors

Elva's phone buzzed with a Facebook notification. Mary had just commented, "Writing a book? I'm so proud of you!" She fondly reminisced about the early days of her career when her boss Mary had mentored her.

Elva remembered how her presentation to the team went terribly wrong one day. Her slides had been packed with all she knew, with font sizes so small that the audience couldn't read. Taken aback, Mary had introduced the then young Elva to Guy Kawasaki's 10-20-30 rule on presentations: Prepare 10 slides. Take 20 minutes. Ensure all text is in 30-point size. Elva followed Guy's dictum. Her next presentation won much appreciation.

In the next two years, Mary mentored Elva in many ways. Elva learned about the people in the organization who wielded real power and influence. She learned from valuable books Mary recommended on crucial soft skills such as servant leadership, negotiation, engaging sponsors, and so on.

The project manager felt grateful for Mary's valuable guidance and mentoring. She could not imagine how her career would have panned out without her mentor's generosity.

Many years flew by. Elva's employer WeWin Associates had just hired a new batch of trainees. One of them, Vishal, was assigned to her team. Though new to the city, the youngster was bright, read voraciously, and was curious to learn new things.

Elva had a knack for spotting hidden talent. She had gained a reputation as an able mentor due to her helpful nature.

As Vishal entered Elva's cubicle one day, he saw a poster that read, "Mentoring is a brain to pick, an ear to listen, and a push in the right direction – John C. Crosby." The poster had a background picture of a Tibetan monk preaching his disciple.

Like the latest car model, I booked my mentoring slot four months ago!!!

And we're still standing in line!

Believe me... It's fully worth the wait!

One is never left wondering with the right mentor!

Vishal quickly proved to be an impressive performer. However, he felt uncomfortable when it came to interacting with his colleagues. Coming from a small town, he did not understand the lingo spoken by city men and women. When his colleague Maggie called him to join her for a coffee in the cafeteria, his mouth dried up. He was unable to give a reply. Noticing the strange expression on Vishal's face, she left.

Elva observed Vishal from a distance. She instinctively understood that if his interpersonal skills did not improve, he would face obstacles in career growth. She resolved to mentor the youngster.

As Vishal was sipping his coffee in the cafeteria one day, Elva asked him whether she could join him. She started the conversation by asking Vishal about his interests. Vishal said he liked reading books and was eager to learn about new technology. He excitedly mentioned a few sites such as Github and TechCrunch from which he was learning new things every day. Elva was impressed. She told him, "I'm going to be your mentor. Feel free to ping me on anything you need."

Elva continued to have these informal chats with Vishal twice every week. Initially, Vishal was shy, but then gradually opened up. He let go of inhibitions eventually, and one day, Elva deliberately asked Maggie to invite him again for a chat over coffee. This time, Vishal smiled. He joined Maggie.

Elva smiled too. She was helping a youngster progress in his career. The wheel had turned 360 degrees!

EXPERT INSIGHTS

Ivo M. Michalick Vasconcelos MSc, PMP, PMI-SP, ACC, CPCC

Executive Director (Brazil), Practical Thinking Group.

Projects in Argentina, Brazil, Chile, European countries, Peru, South Korea, USA. **Industries:** Defence, Energy, Government, Logistics, Mining, Telecommunications.

29+ years. Coaching and mentoring, soft skills, creating PMOs, delivery, governance, international/multicultural projects. PMI volunteer for 12+ years.

The right mentor can make a huge positive difference. I firmly believe that for a mentor–mentee relationship to work, the following elements are essential:

1. *Both parties are open and engaged in the process. The mentee needs to WANT to be mentored by a particular mentor at a specific moment of his life.*

2. *The mentor must keep in mind that every personal journey is unique. He needs to provide space for the mentee to create his path, offering him help and advice along the way.*

3. *All good things come to an end, and most of the time it is up to the mentor to recognize his work is done so both can move forward.*

Ilango Vasudevan PgMP, PMP, AFBCI, CSCP, PMI-ACP

Head, SARAS Analytics (Business Continuity and Program Management Advisory).

Projects in India, Bahrain, GCC, Iran, Mongolia, Sudan, USA. **Industries:** Government, Supply Chain.

20 strong years program/project management serving client initiatives related to business and technology strategy.

There is no "one-size-fits-all" approach to mentoring. It helps to thoroughly customize to the context. Mentoring success also requires you to be tough, demanding, and disciplined.

As a mentor, I took calculated risks by letting my mentees lead from the front in certain critical project situations, despite always holding larger control over the situation. I focused on enhancing every mentee's capability, skill, and career. Mentees, in turn, added much-needed project management expertise to my projects, a win-win and mutually rewarding situation.

My success was a result of mentoring by some of the finest professionals. The best way I could repay them would strive to be the best mentor I can be to my project's team members.

KEYS TO SUCCESS

- Mentors play an invaluable role in career growth and project success.
- Mentors can develop your leadership skills. They can provide valuable advice on your strengths and areas where you need to improve.
- Mentors can help you navigate the complexities of a new organization regarding the power structure, processes, potential challenges, and so on. They can help you open doors which you cannot open yourself.
- Actively seek mentors. Be receptive to their suggestions.
- Make sure that you too mentor your team members to help them grow.
- Mentoring is particularly useful to team members moving to agile projects from the waterfall or hybrid models.

06 What, Why, Who, When, and How

"How can I satisfy them all, pa? If I have to communicate to different stakeholders all day, how can I do any work? They're always asking me for status reports. These people are so unreasonable!" Mano was venting her frustration to her dad as she rode an Uber cab to work.

Mano was taken aback when the cab driver turned to her and said, "Sorry to intrude, but do you work as a project manager?"

Puzzled by the question she asked, "But, how would you know?"

"Young lady, I've felt the same pain. I recently retired as project manager."

He continued, "I didn't want to sit at home and rot watching TV all day. I drive a cab primarily so I can meet interesting people! May I offer you some advice from my experience?"

Mano was very interested. "I'm all ears, sir," she said eagerly.

"Call me Joe. Do you have a plan on how you communicate with your stakeholders?"

"Of course, Joe. Our company has a standardized template that we use for all projects. I copied and pasted it for my project too."

Joe sighed and said, "Every project is different. Every group of stakeholders has different needs. If a client were given a monthly status report when they needed the information weekly, there would be total dissatisfaction! Applying the same template to all projects is a recipe for disaster!"

Joe explained how he had achieved significant success by reaching out to stakeholders early in the project to understand their communication needs. He would ask the questions: What information do you need? How frequently? How should I deliver it? Should it be face-to-face discussions, audio or video calls, emails, or printed reports?

"You have reached your destination." Google Maps interrupted Joe's words of advice. They had already reached Mano's office. Joe said he would be happy to share the rest of his success secrets over the phone during the weekend.

Mano promptly called Joe on Saturday. He said, "Collate and analyze the info requirements. You will quickly find that that the needs are so many that your project team cannot satisfy them all. Also, some information can't be shared due to confidentiality reasons."

How did Joe tackle this situation? He said that he would hold frank discussions with stakeholders conveying his challenges. Along with his team, he would ask the question "why" for every need. This would help stakeholders to prioritize their needs. A customized plan would be created and circulated once agreements had been reached.

The customized approach worked like a charm. Collecting stakeholder views conveyed the fact that the project team was eager to listen, rather than the usual "This is how we will communicate. Take it or leave it!"

Periodically, Joe worked with the major stakeholders to analyze whether the plan was working. They would agree to add, modify, and delete information as needed. The frequency of reports or the media to be used would be updated.

"Try the approach Mano," Joe concluded. "It used to work for me. There's no reason it won't work for you too!"

Mano thanked Joe for his generous advice.

Back at work, she started implementing the new approach. It gave great results. Her approach began to be used by other project managers as well.

Mano thought of how frustrated she had been when she spoke to her father the other day. She was relieved that all that was now history. She thanked her lucky stars for meeting Joe in that Uber cab!

⬟ EXPERT INSIGHTS

Syed Nazir Razik MBA, ACP, CSM

Program Director, Eli India Pvt. Ltd.

Projects in Nation of Brunei, Hong Kong, India, Malaysia, Singapore, Thailand, Turkey, UAE, USA. **Industries:** Agriculture, E-commerce, Healthcare, Information Technology, Logistics, Web Development.

20+ years of experience in developing products and solutions in SMAC, machine learning, and UAV domain. Social media strategist, PMI Agile, VP – Marketing PMI Chennai Chapter. PMI Volunteer since 2008.

Of the 52 project keys, team communication will certainly be in the top five.

Today's multi-generation, multi-cultural and geographically distributed teams with remote workers make communication extremely complex. Corporates constantly grapple with the VUCA (Volatile, Uncertain, Complex and Ambiguous) phenomenon.

The need of the hour is a clear communication management plan incorporating the right combination of content, form, frequency, and medium of communication.

Thanks to technological convergence and interconnectivity, today's organizations and teams are adopting more vibrant tools like Slack, Hangout, Skype, Dialers, and WhatsApp where the response is NOW (faster) and WOW (shorter).

Understanding stakeholders and their needs are the first steps. The "inspect and adapt" approach helps fine-tune the effectiveness of the medium and message. Such a communication plan is critical to maintain business agility and support a collaborative work environment.

Fabio Rigamonti Eng., PMP

Project and Process Change Manager, ECSA Group.

Projects in Italy, Netherlands, Spain, Switzerland, UK. **Industry:** Information Technology.

15+ years of experience in project management and ERP-implementation, leading multicultural teams across Europe; currently based in Switzerland building a PMO. A PMI Leadership Institute Master Class alumnus and volunteer for the PMI Ethics Member Advisory Group. Managed IT projects with consultants and team members from all over Europe with the support of resource centers based in Asia.

Project professionals know that an extensive part (up to 90%) of their work is spent in communicating. This is especially critical in large projects with distributed and virtual teams; in such environments, it is essential to building a proper communication plan, which considers:

- *Experience and roles: Not all team members may have the same level of skill in large project communications.*

- *Time zones: Critical when you need to provide information to a team that will need to provide scheduled deliveries when the project manager and the business analysts are not reachable.*

- *Cultures: Ensure that communications are respectful and constructive; don't forget that some cultures are more direct while others aren't. As such, always rely on formal written communication.*

KEYS TO SUCCESS

- Effective communication is a top critical success factor for project success.
- As a project manager, a good portion of your time is utilized for stakeholder engagement.
- Many projects use a templated approach to stakeholder communication. This approach does not work on every project as stakeholders' communication needs vary.
- Start by reaching out to stakeholders to document their communication needs. Ask them what information is needed, by whom, at what frequency and in what form it should be communicated (What, Who, When, and How).
- Often, the stated needs far exceed what your team can deliver. Ask "Why" for each requirement and prioritize. Negotiate effectively and finalize requirements.
- Circulate the customized, comprehensive plan to all stakeholders.
- Periodically review effectiveness of communications and implement any corrective actions.

Welcome Changes

Astra Constructions was a rapidly growing infrastructure company. It was hiring aggressively to meet new project demands.

The rapid growth was making the task of maintaining records with Excel sheets unwieldy and time-consuming. To tackle these challenges, Tasneem, Astra's Vice President of Human Resources, had decided to implement a PeopleSoft HR system.

Beating out several other bidders, VS Consulting (VSC) won the contract for Astra's PeopleSoft implementation.

VSC realized that rolling out a sophisticated automation system in an infrastructure company would be challenging. The reason? The project required a significant culture shift and change in employee attitudes. Dominic was handpicked to lead the project on VSC's behalf. His excellent change management skills were a key factor in his appointment.

Tasneem introduced Dom to her team. She asked them to extend him all possible cooperation to make the project a success. Dom requested a manager's level meeting soon to acquaint everyone with the project's vision.

Employees of Astra's HR team naturally felt apprehensive. They felt that Tasneem had not consulted them about the project's feasibility. Chris, one of the senior managers, felt that the program would reduce his importance in the department. He started spreading baseless rumors that the project's success was against their interests since one of the project's objectives was to reduce the team by one-third.

Dom soon organized a project kick-off meeting. As a change management expert, he fully knew that people are generally uncomfortable with change. Dissent and fears about the results of change were common. He also knew of the rumors that were being floated about a reduction in team size.

In his early days as project manager, Dom used to ignore people who challenged the project. Believing that they would ask difficult questions and spread negativity, he often wouldn't invite them to stakeholder meetings. This approach had backfired badly. Opponents to the project turned even more suspicious and inimical. They had virtually derailed the project.

Dom would not let history repeat itself. He invited Chris to attend the kick-off meeting with all team members.

Colorful posters explaining project benefits were displayed all around the conference room. HR staff was intrigued by these posters. It appeared their work would actually become easier and more enjoyable. More people would be hired. It seemed that the rumors of staff cuts were unfounded.

Dom started the meeting with a slide that read, "Everyone wants to progress, but no one wants to change." He asked Astra's HR team members, "How often have you been frustrated when an accident or diversion forced you off the regular route on your commute to work? I understand that change is not easy. However, our project's vision is to reduce manual work and errors. You can use the time saved to create programs for a more motivated, engaged workforce!"

Several questions were raised: Will this project lead to me losing my job? What other damage can this project cause me? Will the project make my job tougher or easier?

Empathetic to the fact that the questions were prompted by human resistance to change, Dominic answered every query with candor.

Next, the project's Change Champion was announced. It was Chris! Everyone was surprised. They wondered what had changed. They did not know that Dom had engaged Chris in several one-on-one meetings to address the Astra HR manager's concerns.

With apprehensions effectively managed, Astra's HR team extended their full cooperation. Intense stakeholder engagement ensured project success.

Satisfied, Dom moved to the next project with even greater confidence!

 EXPERT INSIGHTS

Mustafa Hafizoglu PMP

Project Director at SDT Space & Defence Technologies; President – PMI Turkey Chapter.

Projects in European countries, Malaysia, South Korea, Turkey. **Industries:** Aerospace & Defence, Electronics, Manufacturing.

18 years creating PMOs, program and project management, portfolio management, and change management. PMI volunteer (Core Committee Member of PMI's Practice Guide for Governance of Program, Portfolio, and Project); Coauthor of the book *Project Management Analytical Approaches*.

To manage change, we should understand its nature, where it may emerge, and our approach towards it.

We as human beings are programmed not to change since we hang on to what has worked in the past. Realizing the need for change may emerge either from outside or from within the project. Are you ready to kill your project if your company changed its vision and the output of your project will not help the company to reach that vision anymore? Your approach to coping with change is critical. Will using Change Control Boards (CCBs) help you make the right decisions? Not always!

As a project manager, you should create the right environment where each team member has a proactive rather than a reactive approach to changes. Believe me: These steps will contribute strongly to project success.

Mahendiran Periyasamy PMP, CSM, CSP, CSPO, PMI-ACP, ITIL, ICC Certified
agile Coach

Founder & CEO, Energile Consultancy Services LLC.

Projects in Canada, Egypt, Europe, India, Malaysia, Singapore, UK, USA.
Industries: Aeronautical, Finance, Healthcare, Insurance, Manufacturing, Mortgage, Telecommunications.

20+ years of rich experience as certified agile coach, agile transformation consultant, lead trainer, speaker, startup entrepreneur, IT strategist, corporate catalyst with PM excellence.

As project managers and leaders (with or without titles), we are here to make the world better. Through the right thoughts, intentions, and carefully and compassionately chosen actions, each of us can transform the world in a positive way. Change is a natural process of evolving. I see the word "change" ends with two letters, "ge," which I consider to be an acronym for growth engine. Any change can have the effect of a growth engine to achieve bigger and better results. The word challenge also has the word "change" in it. When we look at it in the right perspective, any challenge in our day-to-day life, when applied with the right changing agility mindset, will take us toward greater growth. Hence managing and leading change always drives us toward managing and leading growth. It is not just "going with life," but "growing with life" by transforming lives.

KEYS TO SUCCESS

- Projects bring about change, and people are generally apprehensive about change.
- Your stakeholders are likely to be suspicious and even fear the change that your project may bring about.
- If you neglect these stakeholders concerns, you may be jeopardizing the chance of your project's success.
- Proactively invest time in understanding and allaying your stakeholder's concerns.
- Employ effective and transparent communications as this can go a long way in clarifying concerns.
- Understand that agile teams welcome change, even at late stages. They revel in harnessing change to help the customer develop a competitive advantage.

08 Vault Over That Waterfall

Ganesh was dumbfounded as he received his latest performance appraisal rating. His rating was below reasonable expectations. His team had worked day and night to complete a sophisticated Customer Relationship Management (CRM) project for Prestige Clubs. All requirements had been flawlessly met within time and below the original budget.

Ganesh wondered why he had not been able to retain his top rating of the past year. To clear the air, he scheduled a meeting with his boss Richard.

Richard said that he believed Ganesh deserved the highest rating. However, Julio, the customer representative from Prestige Clubs, had provided strong negative feedback on the project. Richard said, "Julio was very upset with your team's inflexibility. He stated that many new requirements were turned down since your team froze requirements early. Prestige felt that the final product did not entirely match their requirements."

A confused Ganesh explained how the customer's new requirements came so late that there was no room to redesign their databases. Richard was empathetic, but said, "Those are valid reasons. But, customer delight is critical. You didn't delight Prestige!"

Ganesh knew that he could not afford to risk another second-level rating next year, as that would affect his career prospects. He turned to his long-time mentor Moshe, a veteran project manager with whom he had worked with in Israel. Explaining the challenges he was facing, he wondered whether the veteran could give him any pointers.

Moshe asked, "Have you tried agile techniques in your projects?"

Ganesh replied, "I was under the impression that the agile and waterfall methodologies don't mix!"

"That's a common misconception, Ganesh! Several agile techniques can significantly help improve success rates in waterfall projects." He listed a few techniques which he firmly believed would help:

1. Breaking projects into manageable phases helps teams collect requirements over a period rather than all at once. This way, waterfall projects can increase their flexibility.

2. Adopting planning poker helps teams to develop better estimates, increases team buy-in, and boosts morale.

3. User stories, written in plain English, help customers clarify requirements before you travel too far down the road with a faulty design.

4. Increased customer engagement helps teams define requirements and challenges quickly.

5. Waterfall project teams often waste much time in long, unproductive meetings. Agile projects use short stand-up sessions where everything that counts gets conveyed quickly and effectively.

Implementing agile techniques in the next project wasn't easy for Ganesh due to the learning curve of a team steeped in waterfall technique. However, with sustained efforts, he started achieving tangible improvements.

Equipped with over 15 months of phased delivery experience over his next two projects, he attained the prestigious credential, Agile Certified Practitioner (PMI-ACP®).

He had certainly enabled his team to be far more nimble, flexible, and agile!

 # EXPERT INSIGHTS

 ## Jesse Fewell B.S. (Mathematical Sciences)

Author, Speaker, Coach in Agile Project Management.

Projects in Brazil, Canada, China, Egypt, France, India, Malaysia, Netherlands, UAE, UK, USA. **Industries:** Biometrics, Consulting, Defence, Marketing, Research and Development, Tourism.

18+ years. Writer, coach, and trainer in innovation and agile methods. In addition to speaking for Agile, Scrum, and PMI conferences, helped teams across the world deliver products faster with higher quality. A leader in the advancement of management practices, he co-created the PMI-ACP® Agile certification and co-authored PMI's Agile Practice Guide. The world's only certified Project Management Professional® (PMP) to also hold the expert-level agile designations of Certified Scrum Trainer® (CST), and Certified Collaboration Instructor (CCI)®.

Many of us have been told agile approaches are an all-or-nothing collection of techniques. However, true agility is defined by the agile manifesto, a collection of project values that can benefit any project using any methodology.

For example, the value of "individuals and interactions" means leaders can delegate more discretion, even on a fixed-scope project.

Meanwhile, "customer collaboration" means a full-time business representative can clarify confusing requirements, even toward a single delivery.

Finally, we can "respond to change" of scope even with a globally distributed project of part time people.

Do not fall into the trap of only-this and only-that. A little agile can help anyone.

Sivaram Athmakuri PMP, PMI ACP, PMI-PBA, CSP, CSM, CSPO

Agile/Scrum coach, business problem solver.

Projects in Bangladesh, India, Singapore, UAE, UK, USA. **Industries:** Consulting, Education, Government, Healthcare, Information Media, Information Technology, Petrochemicals, Pharmaceuticals.

Independent consultant with 20+ years of industry experience. Conducted 500+ classroom and online sessions on Project Management, Risk Management, Microsoft Project, Agile/Scrum, Lean, and so on.

- *The biggest challenge we face in the ever-changing world of projects is that only 30 percent of what we deliver is consumed. Additionally, too many compelling changes at the last minute can lead to exponential cost overrun. Following agile practices such as iteration review (e.g., every 15/30 days) with potential end users can address the above challenge, killing two birds with one stone.*

- *Millennials are willing to run the extra mile if they find true meaning in their work. When product owners (business) convey their requirements directly to the entire team, they become truly self-managed and proactive. Techniques such as estimation with the whole team will create a motivated workplace.*

- *Quality is the responsibility of the entire team, not just QA. Practices like test-driven development help in achieving error-proof deliverables.*

KEYS TO SUCCESS

- Many project managers are now exploring how to juxtapose the agile and waterfall methodologies.

- You can effectively leverage agile techniques in your projects that use the waterfall methodology.

- You can adopt many techniques. However, these five are exceptionally useful: Phased delivery, increased customer engagement, user stories, planning poker, and stand-up meetings.

- Phased delivery allows your team to break work down into manageable chunks.

- By increasing customer engagement, you are able to quickly and continuously understand their needs.

- User stories help you to clarify client requirements quickly and where required apply fixes early.

- You can engage your teams and get better estimates using planning poker.

- Stand-up meetings help you save time and communicate more effectively.

Fight for What Is Right

Oh no, a delayed flight again! Mike had just been informed at the check-in counter of a two-hour delay due to poor weather. He decided to watch the UEFA Champions league game in the comforts of the premium lounge.

As he was moving to the lounge, Mike's eyes lit up. He had just spotted Professor Ranjit Sharma who had taught Advanced HR during his MBA course. After exchanging pleasantries, the professor explained that he had a long layover on the way back home. He asked how Mike's career was going.

Mike was happy to share with Professor Sharma that he was now managing large projects for a leading tech firm. He then asked the professor a question that had lingered in his mind for long. "In a resource-starved world, it's next to impossible to combine a great leader and a terrific team. If you were forced to choose, what would you prefer? A great team with a mediocre leader or an average team with a remarkable leader?"

Professor Sharma smiled and said, "There's no easy answer! I'm fairly sure that neither combo can deliver project success."

Mike continued. "Our firm made big investments in practical leadership workshops. We now have a bunch of excellent project managers who lead well. However, they find it difficult to succeed with teams that lack the necessary experience and skills. What are we to do?"

The professor agreed that assembling the best project team was a critical success factor. He showed Mike an article he had favorited on his iPad. "How to Pick Project Team Members," authored by Beth Winston, read: "If you get it right, you can immensely improve both the efficiency of the project and its outcome. You need to have the right mix of skills, passion, and attitude to ensure the project gets done with minimum friction and maximum effectiveness."

Mike was interested to know more. The professor cautioned Mike that severe resource crunches and fights for talent were widespread both in the industry and within organizations. It was, therefore, next to impossible for any single project to assemble the best team. He summarized the best practices that a group of his students had recently developed for an MBA assignment:

a. Develop excellent rapport with the HR team.

b. Prioritize the roles where you cannot compromise on quality.

c. Be clear about the skills and qualities you need.

d. Communicate clearly with HR.

e. Do not accept the wrong people.

f. Work hard to build the right team chemistry.

Professor Sharma said that for top priority roles, it was critical for project managers to identify people with an ideal mix of qualities such as technical expertise, emotional

We won because we fought for &
got the BEST talent!
Other teams only got the REST!

quotient, communication skills, willingness to learn, and attention to detail.

He added, "Look for at least three of these in every member of the project team. Not everybody can have the same skill mix. A combination of competencies in the team gives you the flexibility to assign the right roles to the right people. make sure you avoid overly abrasive and unethical individuals.

Two hours went by, and it was time to board. Mike thanked his professor for his valuable insights and practical advice.

 EXPERT INSIGHTS

Rahul Sudame PMI-ACP, CSP, SAFe SPC

Agile Program Manager, Persistent Systems.

Projects in India and USA. **Industries:** Financial Services, Insurance.

18 years of rich experience in project, program management, and agile/process transformation.

Friends, have you gone through a situation, where you on-boarded a team member to match the requirement of the project but then had to spend sizable time in handling or controlling that team member?

One of the lessons I have learned is to wait and fight for a team member with the right attitude rather than onboarding anyone in haste.

An organization or project transitioning to the Agile methodology can be successful only if its team members exhibit the right mindset. In such a case, it becomes critical for the project manager to choose team members focused on teamwork rather than individual heroism. The success of the project (and peace of mind for the project manager) starts with selecting the right team members.

Archana Raghuram B.E. (Computer Science)

Former Global Head of Cognizant's CSR Program.

Projects in Argentina, Australia, Belgium, Brazil, China, El Salvador, Germany, Hungary, India, Ireland, Lithuania, Malaysia, Netherlands, Poland, Philippines, Singapore, Spain, Sweden, Switzerland, UAE, UK, USA. **Industry:** Information Technology.

21+ years of experience, CSR, volunteer program management, project management, corporate communications. Winner of the *Forbes India* philanthropy award in the "Good

Samaritan" category. Honored as "One of the 100 Most Creative People in Business" by *Fast Company* magazine.

Focus on getting the right people into your team. The right attitude and passion are critical.

Putting together a dream team may not always be in your hands, but bringing out the best in them is certainly in the hands of you, the leader.

I recently read an article[1] about Project Aristotle, a Google research study on patterns in high-performing teams. The article discussed the concept of psychological safety, which means "a team climate characterized by interpersonal trust and mutual respect in which people are comfortable being themselves." It is up to us, the leaders, to build this climate. If you can do this, it is possible to make even an average team do wonders.

KEYS TO SUCCESS

- Project success is more probable when you combine a great leader with the best possible team. However, a severe shortage of the right talent could pose a problem.
- Prioritize the key project roles where you cannot compromise on skills and experience.
- Look for a combination of competence that you can mix and match across various activities for project benefit.
- Build bridges with HR and actively negotiate for the best possible team.
- Avoid individuals with poor attitude or a track record of disruptive and unethical behavior.
- In agile projects, you will need team members who display initiative and take responsibility. Actively look for these qualities when you put together your agile team.

---

[1] http://www.huffingtonpost.com/susan-steinbrecher/4-simple-phrases-that-ins_b_9691798.html

10 The Many Faces of Change

John was brimming with confidence. Just back from a marketing call, the Chief Marketing Officer of Innotech was sure that one more large deal for the firm's FMWare product was about to be closed.

Since Dom, the firm's Development Director had already left for the weekend; he approached Mitch of the development team. "Mitch, want to be part of a $850K win? Our client wants 'powder blue' as the background color of all reports. The client wants this done by Monday. For a whiz like you, this should be a breeze!"

Mitch, who had just joined Innotech, was thrilled to help. A contribution to this deal would be a great start to his new job. He said, "Hey, that's awesome! Consider it done."

Although the change looked simple, Mitch knew it involved hundreds of reports and doing it manually was just out of question given the time constraint. Thinking smart, he modified a small piece of code which was executed before every report was loaded. After quickly testing the most-used reports, he demonstrated the change to John. The CMO was delighted. They were both going to enjoy the weekend!

On Wednesday next week, Mitch was shocked to hear from Dom that John was now blaming him for a large lost order. Mitch wondered what had changed in just a few days. He went up to Dom and narrated his Friday evening meeting with John and told him that the change was carried out based on the CMO's request. He added, "Dom, I checked all the main reports. The change worked fine."

Dom explained that the seemingly simple change had somehow caused the software to load extremely slowly during John's demo. "You rushed, Mitch. Despite the minor nature of the change, you should have asked John to submit a formal Change Request (CR) to be considered by the project's Change Control Board (CCB)."

The Director added that the best CCBs included members from various functional areas. As a group, they therefore, had the knowledge and skills to consider all possible impacts of the CR. Several factors were considered, including scope, time, cost, quality, procurement, and communication implications. The CCB would also carry out a cost–benefit analysis of the risk-reward ratio of every CR.

This book on 25 tips to manage Change Control Boards is amazing!!!

Oh! It has now changed to 26 tips... The CCB approved one more way last week!

An effectively staffed CCB helped the project in many ways. Besides acting as a safety buffer between the customer and the team, they also gave project teams valuable inputs in terms of time and value analyses.

On Friday, Mitch had thought he was innovative and responsive to a customer need. He now realized the dangerous effect of acting on changes in haste. He had learned a valuable lesson that would stand him in good stead in the future.

EXPERT INSIGHTS

Rami Kaibni B.Sc. Engineering, PMP

Senior Projects and Development Manager, Field & Marten Associates, Canada.

Projects in Canada, China, Qatar, Palestine, UAE. **Industries:** Academic, Construction (Residential, Commercial, Industrial), Healthcare, Oil and Gas.

13+ years diversified expertise in project and construction management, and real estate development. PMI volunteer since 2015 with an 85% influence rating on projectmanagement. com.

Some changes or often many are inevitable during a project's lifecycle. While some are mandatory, others might be the team's ideas on positive project impact. From my experience, I believe:

1. *The CCB adds value by looking at all aspects of the proposed/requested change. They examine, evaluate, and determine the best course of action and help foster those ideas that can provide a positive impact.*

2. *Always educate stakeholders about the CR process. Keep them informed of the possible effects of changes and get their endorsement.*

3. *Maintain a detailed log of CRs with the course of action recommended and impacts on the project. This log is invaluable for future projects as lessons learned: (a) to minimize/avoid changes that could affect similar projects; (b) add value by adopting relevant changes during the design phase.*

Amitava Banerjee B.Com, Postgraduate Diploma in Marketing Management

Regulatory Affairs Manager, Reliance Jio.

Projects in India. **Industries:** Not-for-Profits, Service, Telecommunication.

14+ years of experience in government telecom projects, regulatory, service operation. Founder Member of the PMI West Bengal Chapter (PMI-WBC). Currently volunteering as Director-Finance with PMI-WBC. Conference Director, Project Management Regional Conference, Kolkata, 2017.

Telecommunication projects require critical attention to time management since contract terms in government projects specify severe liquidated damages for delayed delivery. This means a project that is significantly delayed is almost certainly a failure on the profitability front too.

With numerous stakeholders involved, we frequently receive requests for plan changes.

Since changes can kill our schedule, we invest time and effort in setting up the right mix of people in our CCBs. We also work closely with our CCBs to very carefully evaluate and review customer-originated change requests for time and cost impact.

Based on CCB decisions and directions, we hold proactive discussions with customers. These steps have helped us save significant amounts by avoiding liquidated damages and hence improve project success rates.

KEYS TO SUCCESS

- Change is an integral part of projects. Without change, there would be no need for project management.
- Project teams should include experienced team members who can analyze and understand all potential impacts of change. By appropriately ascertaining the impact of change requests (CRs), team members help to mitigate serious risks.
- Change Control Boards (CCBs) are most effective when they are staffed with the right mix of people from various areas. Significant benefits they provide are:
  - ➢ Act as a change management buffer between the team and the client.
  - ➢ Help the project team analyze all possible impacts of change.
  - ➢ Provide the team valuable buffer time, helping them develop the right strategy to deal with the change.
- CCBs carefully evaluate and review customer-originated change requests for time, cost, and the scope affected impacts.
- CCBs help project teams by giving them time cushions to analyze changes.
- Having the right people on your project's CCB is critical to making sure that CRs are effectively handled.

Vendor or Friendor?

11

It was 8 p.m. on the eve of the prestigious project management conference. Delegate kits were being assembled with conference bags, pens, writing pads, and sponsor brochures for 1,200+ attendees. Thirty volunteers were keen on completing the job early to prepare themselves for the big day. The team had been planning and preparing for over ten months for this day.

Using a factory assembly line approach, they efficiently stuffed the conference kits. Mano, the conference chairperson, and a volunteer herself, was there, giving the team a hand. She was excited by the team's energy and speed and thought the task would be complete in an hour.

"Oh God!" she heard someone exclaim. "The badge vendor has messed up. They didn't perforate. Attendees will find it hard to detach the food coupons. What can we do? Less than 12 hours left!"

Mano wouldn't let her anxiety show. She said, "Let's not panic. I'm sure we can find a solution."

Robert, one of the youngest in the team, came up with a great idea: Buy a few sets of box-cutters and rulers from a nearby store. Apply just enough pressure to the cards to score them. The suggestion was accepted.

Cutters and rulers were purchased. Mano and five other volunteers stayed back, confident that they could get the job done on time. Joining them was Sathya, head of Eventures, the event management firm that had won the contract to help run the conference. Picking up a box cutter and ruler himself, he started scoring badges.

Mano was pleasantly surprised. She told him, "Sathya, This goof-up wasn't your firm's fault. There's no need at all for you to score name tags!"

Sathya's reply thrilled the chairperson. "Mano, you told me that your team was the customer and mine the vendor only till the contract was awarded. After that, you said, we would all be one team, working together to deliver the best possible conference. It doesn't matter which vendor slipped up. I'm just a team member helping fix the issue!"

Mano remembered that conversation well. As a project manager, she had learned from work experience that vendors actively contributed to project success when they were treated as valued partners. Vendor-related risks were substantially reduced. She had observed that the opposite happened with her colleagues who extracted the last penny from every deal. When they adopted the attitude "I'm the customer; you better do what I say," results were rarely good.

Mano usually negotiated fair deals with all vendors with help from her team. She ensured that every vendor was treated respectfully and as a valued team member. On occasions where scope had increased, she made sure vendors were compensated fairly.

Those efforts were paying off now and how! Sathya was going beyond his contract terms to help the volunteer team. Not stopping just with tags, the Eventures team contributed in many other ways to make the conference very successful.

Every member of Mano's volunteer team learned a valuable lesson on managing vendors. They would go on to apply this success secret to their projects too.

"Oh, we treat them not just as a 'vendor' but as a 'friendor'!"

 ## EXPERT INSIGHTS

Daisy Ruiz Diaz Lovera Bachelors in Mechanical Engineering, Masters in Production Engineering, Business and Strategic Management, PMP

Consultant, allaboutXpert, Australia.

Projects in: Australia, Brazil, Paraguay, USA. **Industries:** Education, Information Technology, ITES, Mining, Oil and Gas.

Experienced project, program, and portfolio management (P3M) professional. Rich experience in strategic management of business and projects in multinational organizations across several industries and in multicultural environments. Graduate of PMI's Leadership Institute Master Class (LIMC) 2012. Volunteer and volunteer leader with the Project Management Institute (PMI).

Most complex projects involve significant contributions from vendors and contractors.

Often, project managers take the phrase "the customer is king" literally. Vendors are not treated with the respect they deserve and are expected to dance to the project team's tunes. This is a dangerous strategy. People treated with disrespect are unlikely to perform at their best. When significant contributors to your project underperform, your project will certainly suffer.

On my projects, I make it a priority to treat vendors and contractors as valued partners. Amazing results are achieved when you share the project's vision with vendors and make them feel like they are an integral part of the project team.

Jayakrishnan P S PMP

Service Delivery Manager, SunTec Business Solutions.

Projects in Europe, Malaysia, Middle East, Singapore, USA. **Industries:** Banking, TTL and Upstream Oil & Gas logistics.

17+ years of in-depth experience in software product delivery and implementation experience. PMI volunteer.

Treat vendors with respect and be fair at all times. While it is the right thing to do, it will also enhance the relationship and bring real results! Communicate this clear message: "Together, we can achieve win-win results!"

Great results are achieved when both sides accomplish their goals. As product vendors, we don't often have competency in all aspects of the business. Expert support from other vendors becomes an imperative. Real success comes when we gain a competitive edge with the assistance of vendors who complement our project in areas outside our core competencies.

Establishing long-term relationships with strategic vendors helps build trust, preferential treatment, and gives us continuous access to their expert knowledge. Availability of fact-based information is essential in taking the right decisions that transform a vendor relationship into a genuine, mutually beneficial partnership.

KEYS TO SUCCESS

- Recognize that your vendors will often fulfill key project requirements for which capability does not exist in your organization.

- Negotiate based on principles and objectives, not on positions. Both parties should win a negotiation.

- Write balanced contracts. If you are going to impose penalties, consider rewards too. At the least, you would have given an opportunity to the vendor to perform and benefit.

- Invest time in cultivating fair dealings with vendors. Make them feel valued for their contributions to your project.

- Conduct vendor appraisals on the lines of employee appraisals. This way you can clearly communicate what you expect, reach agreement, and periodically monitor to avoid unpleasant surprises.

- The "Friendor" attitude will give improved project performance, reduced risk, and therefore greater probability of project success.

12 Mr. Client, You Are Wrong!

"The customer is king. They can do no wrong. Give them what they want. They will be happy, and so will we!" This advice from Elva's boss had seemed entirely plausible then but had ultimately driven the asset management software project to disaster.

Her team's common sense views were overridden by the boss's advice. Elva had followed the client's requirements to a 'T.' When the user interface proved to be woefully non-intuitive, implementation had failed. Elva was made the scapegoat. Competitors to Elva's firm had a field day highlighting this failed project to potential clients.

She firmly resolved then that she would not let that situation repeat.

Elva was appointed project manager for a facility management software project for Galaxy Infra, a leading construction firm. When there was a user requirement to place 49 user entry elements on one screen with no vertical scrolling, her team felt it just wouldn't work. With much of the entered data needing on-screen validation, Elva's team believed this web form would be a nightmare for users.

To make it simpler, the team had suggested that this form be broken up into six sequential screens. However, Milton, the customer representative, was adamant that he would not modify this requirement.

Just back from a conversation with her current boss Emilio, Elva felt déjà vu. She was mulling over Emilio's advice to blindly implement the customer requirement over her team's concern of serious usability issues.

That weekend, Elva was a delegate at an international project management conference. A well-known expert was delivering the keynote, "Sorry, Mr. Client. You Are Wrong!" The speaker stressed how critical it was for PMs to be courageous in challenging clients on invalid assumptions.

"As the solution provider, you know what works. You have scars from past failures. Invest time in convincing the clients. If not, you will hurtle down the slippery slope to failure."

The keynote strengthened Elva's resolve to stay firm with Galaxy Infra on modifying their 49-element one-screen requirement.

Back at work, she spent time researching case studies on simplicity in user interface design. She asked her team members to play the role of devil's advocate. Based on their feedback, she modified her pitch to Galaxy Infra. The team created prototypes of both the complex and simple variations of the screens. They were smart enough to shoot simple videos of actual users navigating through both screens.

At the meeting next week, Elva said, "Milton, we both want this project to succeed. I understand your viewpoint on the 49-element user input form. However, research proves that user interface complexity drastically increases the risk of implementation failure. I've been involved in a few of these failures myself."

She then played the videos her team had prepared. The videos had time stamps showing that the simpler screens could be completed in one-fourth the time when compared to the single complicated screen.

The visual evidence was so stark that Milton was convinced and submitted a change request to accommodate the more straightforward user interface.

"Wow, Elva! You accomplished the impossible!" The team was far more confident of project success now. Elva's stock in the organization skyrocketed after this episode.

EXPERT INSIGHTS

Muhammad A B Ilyas PgMP, PMP, PMI-RMP, PMI-ACP, PMI-SP

CEO, LIFELONG.

Projects in Australia, Arabian Gulf, Egypt, Ghana, India, Indonesia, Iraq, Italy, Lebanon, Malaysia, Nigeria, Philippines, South Africa, Singapore, Spain, Sweden, Turkey, UK, USA. **Industries:** Finance, Government, Investment, Oil and Gas, Professional Services, Telecommunications.

18+ years of experience on projects related to information systems, product development, and corporate governance. 14+ years teaching undergraduate university students. 10+ years of volunteering with PMI.

Using the classification of cultures proposed by Dr. Richard Lewis, project managers from multi-active and reactive cultures risk losing goodwill if they bluntly challenge inputs provided by customers or other stakeholders. This is particularly the case of stakeholders with higher levels of power and influence.

Even in such cultures, the best interests of the project often require that requirements or inputs are not accepted without careful analysis of their consequences. Navigating cultural norms to say NO in a manner acceptable to stakeholders is a skill that distinguishes good project managers from the rest. Awareness of what constitutes tacit acceptance in a given cultural setting is also important to guard against inadvertent scope creep.

Miguel Cotrina MPM, PMP, PMO-CP, CSM, ITIL

CEO and Project Manager, Daccos IT Solutions, Peru.

Projects in France, Mexico, Peru, UK, USA. **Industries:** Consulting, Education, Entertainment, Information Technology, Media, Social Sector.

10+ years in project management, information technology, software engineering, and cloud computing. PMI volunteer since 2009. President at PMI Cajamarca, Peru Chapter (2017–2019). Awarded the honor of outstanding Fulbright Scholar by the US Government.

How do you treat your clients? One of the most effective ways to interact with them is having a good attitude by practicing positive leadership even when we have to say "No."

We can engage more with our clients and improve our communication with them through the 3-to-1 positivity ratio. This means that for every negative emotion, thought or experience, we need at least three positive emotional experiences during our interactions.

As project managers, this approach will help us to foster better relationships with clients to understand their expectations and requirements better as well as to provide real value to them.

Several research studies have also shown that experiencing positive emotions enhance physical and mental health to succeed in personal and professional life.

KEYS TO SUCCESS

- "The customer is king" is a phrase that is usually sacrosanct in project management.
- However, as project manager, you and your organization have a moral obligation to educate clients.
- Where you believe that some expectations are unrealistic, make it a point to communicate clearly and transparently.
- In the case of customers asking for impossible product features, leverage your organization's expertise to explain with case studies.
- You may often find features that can provide the client exceptional value at little or no added cost. Communicate these features, obtain buy-in, and proceed.
- When relevant, be diplomatic and persuasive in communicating better alternatives to customers.
- This attitude earns you customer loyalty and this ultimately builds sustainable, profitable, long-term business partnerships.

Look in the Mirror!

"**D**o You Know You?" was the intriguing name for a leadership workshop for project managers at SolutionsMax, a firm known for implementing innovative IT solutions for pharma companies.

"Thanks, everyone, for completing your homework. I've never had to work so hard to get people to complete their work!" Kim, the facilitator, announced. Many attendees laughed.

Before the workshop, she had asked the participants to fill out a web form listing their strongest and weakest traits. Each would also indicate similar characteristics for every one of their colleagues.

Kim explained her rationale for collecting the data. "We all have distinct strengths and a few weaknesses. Leveraging our strengths and managing our weaknesses will help us be more successful project managers.

"What should you spend more of your time on? Fortifying your strengths or reducing your weaknesses? Let's have a show of hands." Eleven attendees chose fortifying strengths. Nine thought they would like to work on their weaknesses.

Kim stated that neither group was wrong. Fortifying strength could bring quick wins. While reducing flaws was important too, people had to draw the line at some point so that they didn't lose their individuality. "Play to your strengths and work on your weaknesses," Kim exhorted the attendees. "However, be authentic. Don't try to become someone else!"

The trainer also added that there was a third critical area for project managers to consider.

"Let me illustrate with a quadrant." She drew a two-by-two grid on the white board and labeled the four segments "Known Strengths," "Known Weaknesses," "Pleasant Surprises," and "Danger!"

"The first and second quadrants are self-explanatory. The third, 'Pleasant Surprises,' includes those traits you considered weaknesses but others thought were strengths. The fourth quadrant is labeled 'Danger' since it represents blind spots. You think you are strong in these areas, but others consider them as weaknesses. This is a danger zone, and you should invest time in these areas.

"Let's consider the example of Ramnath, a fictional project manager." Kim moved to a slide that showed his top known strength to be the ability to work hard. His known weakness was that he was a poor communicator. Ramnath's pleasant surprise was the fact that he was passionate about his work. His blind spot was his inability to see the big picture.

Over the next few hours, Kim led the team through several group activities that helped them understand themselves. Exciting role-plays helped the project managers understand their strengths and weaknesses.

All of them felt that they had seen themselves in the mirror on the wall and eagerly looked forward to the next monthly session. The PMs were sure they would learn much more.

"Ahem... I don't think this improves your 'strengths'..."

EXPERT INSIGHTS

Naomi Caietti PMP, CTM

Founder and Director, Naomi Caietti Consulting.

Projects primarily in the USA plus over 80 other countries around the world. **Industries:** Communications, Construction, Consulting, Education, Engineering, Finance, Government, Health Care, Information Technology, Insurance, Legal, Nonprofit, Procurement, Publishing, Real Estate, Research & Development, Retail, Transportation.

A sought-after speaker, coach, and published author. Addressed thousands of project managers around the world. 25+ years' corporate experience as a credentialed project manager in public, private, and nonprofit sector focused on managing high-visibility enterprise IT implementations in key industries.

Are you a self-aware project manager? Emotional intelligence (EQ) predicts people's ability to control their emotions, manage other people, and achieve success. Recent research shows it's not your education or intelligence quotient (IQ) that make you successful in your career, but emotional intelligence abilities.

EQ competencies and behaviors are developed through practice, time and experience on tactical and strategic projects. Be ready to switch and shift, uncover your greatest strengths and close behavioral gaps, find a mentor/coach, and network with your community to build relationships to propel your leadership forward.

(Excerpt from article published at ProjectManagement.com in the ProjectsatWork section. Reproduced with permission from the author.)

Paul Pelletier LLB, PMP

Business Owner, Paul Pelletier Consulting Inc.

Projects in Cameroon, Canada, Ethiopia, Tanzania, USA. **Industries:** Insurance, Law, Tourism.

Corporate lawyer, project manager, author, international public speaker, and business executive with over 25+ years of experience in senior roles in government and industry. A recognized global leader in the project management profession. Serves on the Project Management Institute's Ethics Member Advisory Group. Published author of *Workplace Bullying – It's Just Bad for Business.*

To be a respected PM leader, you can't only have expertise and experience – you also need critical soft skills.

Continually upgrading your skills is critical to achieving continuing success. To which skills should you accord top priority?

First, embody a servant leader philosophy and create a respectful, collaborative and nurturing workplace culture. The success of others must drive your passion for serving people. Be as authentic, open and as honest as you can be.

Second, develop negotiation and conflict management skills. Learn to be politically astute. Finding a middle ground that works politically is a skill. Conflict is a natural occurrence in our workplaces. Being strategic during conflicts requires courage, integrity, and independent judgment. My mantra is that we can agree to disagree without being disagreeable.

Leadership skills beat out expertise and experience on the road to PM success – hands down!

KEYS TO SUCCESS

- Leadership is a top trait for project success.
- To be an effective leader, you need to be intensely aware of your strengths and weaknesses.
- Invest in fortifying your strengths.
- Work on reducing your weaknesses too, but don't waste too much time on these areas. Rather, compensate for them by picking team members with strength in these areas.
- Blind spots are dangerous. These are areas where you think you are strong, but others believe you are weak. You need to work on your blind spots.
- Be true to yourself and be authentic.

14   Real Results Matter

"Make a splash. Launch something big to celebrate our silver jubilee next year!" Armed with this mandate from VXL Bank's Board of Directors, the CEO decided on a project to develop and launch a brand new, feature-rich mobile application named "VXLForYou."

InfoVision, a leader in the mobile banking app industry, beat out several competitors to win the contract. Mike was appointed InfoVision's project manager. Working with Dmitri, VXL's CTO, he prepared a charter with the project's high-level scope, cost, schedule, stakeholders, and risks for the project.

Mike's team studied the detailed user requirements in VXL's original request for proposal (RFP). The team designed, developed, and tested a compact twelve-screen app which integrated several of the bank's services.

VXL's IT team tested the app internally. They reported to Dmitri that the app had all the needed features specified in the RFP. Delighted with product quality and speed of delivery, the CTO sent a congratulatory email to the vendor's CEO and Mike's team.

Dmitri's team requested testing and feedback from VXL's executives and a select group of long-time customers. The CTO was confident that he would get very positive feedback.

How wrong he was! Feedback from both customers and bank executives was uniformly negative. The strongest comment came from Tejinder, VXL's head of Consumer Banking. He had checked several competitor bank's apps and found VXLForYou to be extremely difficult to use. The app was uncomfortably slow and lacked important features of other bank apps: combining multiple accounts, tracking investments, and password reset.

When Dmitri said InfoVision had dotted every "i" and crossed every "t," Tejinder smiled and said, "This is like a doctor saying that the surgery was successful, but the patient died anyway!"

Launching the product in its current state would be disastrous.

Mike's team weren't expecting this. They felt they had satisfied every client requirement. The project manager explained to them that merely delivering all scope on time and within budget was not sufficient. They had failed in the critical area of "benefits realization."

While the project was now far behind schedule, Mike was not going to give up easily. He negotiated with Dmitri for a six-month extension. The new launch date would still be during VXL's silver jubilee celebrations. Realizing that some fault still lay with his team, Dmitri consulted with his CEO who approved the extension.

Mike's team worked on a complete rework of the app, carefully listening to the "Voice of the Customer." They gathered requirements and expectations directly from account holders. Kiosks were set up inside several bank branches. Prototypes of app features helped customers provide immediate feedback.

Analyzing feedback and requirements, Mike's team found that customers expected easier ways to transfer money, reset passwords, and ways to track investments made through VXL Bank.

Top priority was accorded to these features. Frequent testing was carried out on prototypes and mockups of new features. Mike's team built the suggestions and improvements into the app.

The hard work paid off when the new app moved to the top lists of downloads on the Play Store and App Store soon after launch. Feedback ratings were uniformly high.

Mike and his team had learned a vital lesson. Listening to the Voice of the Customer and delivering real results were far more important than just delivering all paper requirements on time and within budget!

⬟ EXPERT INSIGHTS

Theofanis Giotis MSc, Ph.D. CSM/CSP, PMP, PMI-ACP, CTT+, ITIL, MCSE, MCT

CEO of 12PM Consulting, Greece.

Projects in France, Greece, UAE, UK. **Industries:** Banking, Construction, Food, Information Technology, Insurance, Media, Pharmaceuticals, Shipping, Telecommunication, Training.

30 years as project, program and portfolio manager, agile coach, instructor, consultant, author, trainer, and entrepreneur. Delivered multiple presentations in global project management congresses. Co-founder and first President of PMI Greece Chapter (2005–2014), Rotarian President (2011–2013), Leader of ScrumAlliance, Agile and Scrum Greek User Group. Involved in 15+ ANSI and ISO standards for project, program, and portfolio management.

Projects, programs and portfolios (PPPs) are selected, initiated, planned, designed, implemented, controlled, and closed by PEOPLE for PEOPLE. If projects, programs, and portfolios DO NOT deliver the indented benefits to stakeholders, then PEOPLE involved in the whole process have failed. Benefits realization is ONLY about stakeholders. So, "If you don't find stakeholders, STAKEHOLDERS will Find YOU LATER..."

If a project fails, you may lose some money... If a program fails, you may lose a lot of money... If a portfolio fails, you may lose your company!

Karen Clarke PMP, MSP Practitioner, Certified Management Consultant (IMCNZ), Certified P3M3 Assessor

Consultant, Karen Clarke Consulting.

Projects in Australia, New Zealand, USA. **Industries:** Banking & Finance, Energy and Utilities, Government, Telecommunications.

25+ years of project and program management experience, establishing PMOs, P3M3 capability assessment, trainer and facilitator, portfolio consultant.

Good governance is the key to achieving benefits.

Project management is the vehicle by which we deliver on organizational strategy. Successful projects, therefore, deliver outcomes and benefits, right? Well, not necessarily. That's because the ultimate goal is delivering business value. And the value to the organization is determined by its senior leadership, which is then required to provide guidance and support to projects to deliver that value.

Long after the project has completed and closed, the quality of the project's governance will have ensured the right outcomes and benefits to be realized, and sustainable change has been achieved.

KEYS TO SUCCESS

- The definition of project success has moved beyond full scope delivered on time and within estimated budgets.
- If you and your team focus primarily on documented requirements, you risk missing the forest for the trees.
- As project manager, you should carefully listen to customer voices to understand expectations and determine whether those expectations can be met.
- You should continuously analyze whether project deliverables will deliver the committed benefits.
- In agile environments, iteration reviews help product owners to showcase working software to end users. During these reviews, users can highlight missing elements that will make the current feature complete. This approach allows for necessary changes to be implemented early and therefore at minimum cost.

Pain First, Gain Next

Dheeraj couldn't contain his excitement. He was pleasantly surprised to have been appointed to head a prestigious new $115 million project to build a premium gated community on the outskirts of the city. An expensive advertisement campaign was already on. Inquiries had started streaming in.

In ten years, Dheeraj had executed four projects of $45 million each. The new project was more than double in size and much larger in scope. It also involved more landscaping, amenities, and roads. Construction for the first of three phases was planned to begin in three weeks. Work was going on for material procurement, site preparation, putting up a front office, and model apartments for prospective customers.

As Dheeraj was grasping the sheer scale of the new assignment, he remembered a very senior manager in the construction industry, Mr. Kaito Tanaka, with whom he had started his career. A much sought-after consultant for many leading real estate companies in the country, Mr. Tanaka was well-known for meticulous planning. Dheeraj decided to get the veteran's advice before starting the project. He fixed a two-hour appointment.

Mr. Tanaka started the conversation with a story. "Dheeraj, do you know the story of the bamboo?"

When Dheeraj replied in the negative, the veteran continued: "The Chinese bamboo plant grows this way. Ample sunlight, regular watering, and careful tending seem to yield no results for almost four years after planting. There is no growth above the ground. After that, in just four weeks, the bamboo shoots up, growing well beyond 50 feet."

"How does this happen?" asked Dheeraj.

"What was going on in the first four years? While there was no visible growth above the ground, the plant was developing strong roots that can hold the weight that a sudden vertical growth would bring."

Mr. Tanaka went on to say, "Let me share a secret. Any project's success begins with meticulous and careful planning."

Dheeraj's first task the next day was to ask his boss to postpone the start of the first phase of construction by five weeks. He explained that his team needed this extra time to thoroughly plan every activity.

"That's impossible!" said the boss. "Your request will delay apartment handing over. These delays will mean massive losses. We'll have to pay compensation to buyers for every day past the dates we committed!"

Dheeraj assured the boss that he knew of the penalty clauses and patiently explained how five extra weeks of planning now might end up saving several weeks in the execution phase. There were back and forth discussions on ifs and buts, but the project manager ultimately got a go-ahead for 27 extra days for planning.

Dheeraj engaged key project stakeholders including external suppliers in planning activities. Getting inputs from everyone in the team, he prepared elaborate schedules with supporting documents. Dates were fixed for completing model apartments in each block. No stone was left unturned.

The team prepared exhaustive plans including detailed time and cost estimates. Dheeraj asked his team to consider all possible project risks. Mohamed, the scheduler, warned that monsoon rains could stop the project for at least 30 to 40 days. All identified risks were factored into the schedule. Dheeraj and his team then came up with at least two response plans for each risk.

Armed with this detailed plan, Dheeraj informed management that the first phase consisting of 512 apartments, villas, and row houses would be completed in 33 months, with a two-month buffer.

Dheeraj ultimately completed the project a full month ahead of schedule and won praise for his amazing and detailed planning skills. He was happy that the initial pain had indeed brought valuable long-term gain!

"You see, he is a meticulous planner!"

⊛ EXPERT INSIGHTS

Shinichi Tasaka PMP, ITIL(F), ITC

Director – Training Services, Management Solutions Co., Ltd.

Projects in Japan. **Industry:** Automotive.

32+ years of rich experience as project manager in the Japanese automotive industry. Expertise in PMO support and project management training.

Volunteer with PMI since 2003. Chair of the Translation Verification Committee of the PMBOK® Guide 5th Edition. Immediate past Secretary General of the PMI Japan Chapter (2010–2015).

Through PMO support services, we try our customer's projects by firmly performing the planning phase of the project, and get successful service in over 80% of them. The PMBOK® guide also states that the planning phase is one of the main project phases. If a good plan is formulated, the success of the project is as good as 90% guaranteed, because the execution phase only needs to proceed according to the baseline chosen in the planning phase, monitor, and correct the deviation from the baseline. If it matches the baseline, it will almost proceed as planned. This is the same as China's bamboo cultivation case.

Upendra Babu Pagadala MCA, CSM, PMP

Infrastructure Project Manager with a global infrastructure organization.

Projects in Australia, India, UAE, USA. **Industries:** Automotive, Business Process Outsourcing, Chemicals, Construction, Information Technology Infrastructure.

Technocrat with over 15 years of experience delivering successful projects in several continents. Deep expertise in IT Infrastructure and enterprise resource planning implementation projects. Creator and moderator of the Facebook project management groups, "Project Manager," "PMP – A Project Manager's First Step," and "PM360."

I often see inexperienced project managers rush into execution with little or no planning.

They are eager to impress sponsors and customers with "quick wins" that demonstrate their ability to hit the ground running. Unfortunately, they don't realize that these quick wins may soon turn into "significant losses" of time and money for reworking the deliverables.

Experience has taught me that detailed planning saves time and money in the long run. However, it takes courage, confidence, and excellent communication skills to convince sponsors that detailed planning also represents progress that ultimately brings results.

The project manager who plans while others rush into execution will ultimately win, just as the slow tortoise did against the rash hare.

KEYS TO SUCCESS

- Invest time and effort in creating detailed plans. Insufficient planning is a top project failure factor.
- Your team members may be tempted to rush into execution with little or no planning. You may do this because you want to show quick wins through deliverables.
- When your plans or assumptions change, those deliverables will need rework, causing your project delays and cost overruns.
- Invest time in convincing stakeholders about the benefits of detailed planning.
- Historical information and lessons learned knowledge bases are a good source to lean on during the planning process.

16 80% Focus on the 20%

Dominic was driving down the scenic route to his parents' farmhouse. After much thought, he had made up his mind to attend the large family get-together. After several stressful weeks at work, he certainly needed to relax!

As he reached the farmhouse, uncle Mariano gave Dominic a broad smile and his trademark bear hug. He said, "Hey, Dom! How's my favorite nephew doing? What's with the fatigued look?"

Admiring his uncle's perceptivity, he replied, "Project management is incredibly stressful. I love what I do, but there always seems to be so much to do in so little time!

"Sometimes I'm pushed into thinking project managers are the world's unluckiest people. We face a seemingly infinite set of challenges. No wonder people say project managers seem to be chained to a treadmill that never stops.

"You know me; I'm very methodical. But in trying to spread my attention across everything in my project, I sometimes miss important things. I end up paying heavily for those misses!"

Having managed the assembly line in a car plant for years, Mariano understood Dom's situation.

Hand over Dom's shoulder, he said, "I can feel your pain. In a stressful assembly line situation, I quickly learned that it is more critical to work smart than work hard. If you try to do everything, you'll spread yourself thin. You need to pick the battles you fight smartly."

Dom knew his uncle meant well but wasn't entirely convinced. He asked, "I understand. But how do I decide which items need my full attention?"

Forming the right words in his mind, Mariano continued: "Do you know the famous Pareto principle? Joseph Juran wrote that excellent results can be achieved with a laser-focus on the 'vital few' over the 'insignificant many.' In your work, I'm sure you've noticed that just one-fifth of your work may take well over three-fourths of project time and use up a large part of your budget."

A spark lit up in Dominic's mind. He thanked his uncle and joined the other family members to relish his mom's famous ravioli.

Back at home on Sunday night, his mind turned to his uncle's advice. He googled for the terms "Project management" and "80-20 rule," and found an Amazon link to the book *The Lazy Project Manager* by Peter Taylor. Reading the book on his Kindle device, he found this useful piece of advice: "By concentrating your project management and learning to exercise effort where it matters, you can learn to work smarter."

Managing the project schedule had been particularly challenging for Dom, with 100+ activities in progress during any two-week period. Analyzing how many of those activities were currently on the project's critical path or near-critical path, he arrived at 24.

"Bingo!" thought Dom. If he focused on these activities, he could give them the high priority they deserved. He would be able to deeply analyze the risks in those activities while delegating the remaining 75+ activities to assistant project managers. They could always escalate serious issues in those tasks to him!

Dom realized that he could follow a similar approach to other factors such as stakeholders, time and cost estimates and so on. Over the next few months, he hardly missed any critical items. Practical application of the 80-20 rule to project management activities had certainly worked wonders for him! Dom's stress levels dropped drastically. In his mind, he thanked his uncle Mariano for valuable advice and thought the decision not to skip the family get-together proved to be golden.

 ## EXPERT INSIGHTS

Adilson Pize PMP, CBPP, PMO-CC, CSM, ITIL Foundation

CEO and Consultant at Excellence Consultants, Writer, Speaker, and Professor in MBA Courses.

Projects in Australia, Bangladesh, Brazil, Canada, Malaysia, Sri Lanka, UK, USA. **Industries:** Apparel, Fashion, Finance, Food and Beverages, Government, Healthcare, Manufacturing.

25+ years. Deep expertise in strategic planning, project management, PMO implementation, business process management, quality management and IT governance. PMI volunteer since 2003. Currently, Member of the Advisory Board of the PMI Rio Grande do Sul Chapter and Ambassador of PMI São Paulo Chapter.

When everything is a priority, nothing is a priority!

Based on experience, I suggest you maintain sharp focus and strong efforts on the highest priority project factors. This principle applies to work packages, risks, stakeholders, vendors, decisions, etc. In prioritizing, you can use a tool such as the "Importance–Urgency" matrix, or define and use other project-specific criteria.

However, prioritizing project aspects alone isn't enough for success! We need to adopt the right strategies to deal with priority factors. Here is an example of the right actions based on the "Importance–Urgency" matrix:

- *High importance and high urgency: just do it.*
- *High importance and low urgency: schedule it.*
- *Low importance and high urgency: delegate/push back.*
- *Low importance and low urgency: don't do it.*

Author's note: Adilson Pize here is referring to Eisenhower's Importance–Urgency Decision Matrix above. Readers will benefit from this diagram that clarifies the concepts above.

	Q1	Q2
IMPORTANT	Crises Deadlines Problems	Goals: Personal, Professional
NOT IMPORTANT	Interruptions Meetings Activities Q3	Distractions Time Wasters Games Q4
	URGENT	**NOT URGENT**

Lily Murariu M. Eng., CDP (Career Development Practitioner), DBA in Project Management

Senior Program Manager in Indigenous and Northern Affairs Canada.

Projects in Canada and Romania. **Industries**: Academia, Banking, Consulting, Manufacturing, and NGO.

24+ years of experience delivering project success in the public sector, governance, risk professional. Member of the boards of directors of the Vocational Rehabilitation Association (VRA), and Project Management Institute (PMI) chapters in Ottawa (ON) and Regina (South SK).

It is impossible for any project manager to do everything. Maximum effectiveness can only be achieved by focusing on the few factors that can deliver maximum impact. Here is what I would do:

- *Focus on the fuzzy-front-end of the lifecycle. Bring along stakeholders and project teams as early as possible to this stage.*

- *Continuously champion the value of planning. Develop competency from within the project, using planning as a retention tool. Allow team members to dream, enjoy the ride, and to walk side by side with you every step of the way.*
- *Develop and promote strategic innovation management, and business technology management (BTM) competencies within your team.*
- *Use lessons learned from others' projects. Don't be terrified of failing. Admit your failure, embrace lessons learned, and ingrain them into the next stage. Grow and mature with your project.*

KEYS TO SUCCESS

- Complex projects usually involve an overwhelmingly large set of elements that are difficult to manage. If you try to manage them all, you will end up spreading yourself thin. Critical elements end up not getting the attention they need, causing serious issues.
- Apply Pareto's 80-20 rule to various categories such as work packages, estimates, stakeholders, risk, procurement, and quality issues.
- For example, you may find that around 20% of ongoing project work packages are on the critical path. Similarly, 20% of estimates may consume a large part of project budget.
- Focus on the 20% of every category that can cause maximum project impact. Delegate the rest.
- Revisit your lists at appropriate intervals since they may change over time.

17 Severe Starting Trouble

Gokul was becoming restless. After poring over paperwork, spreadsheets, and contracts all morning, he was still clueless. As head of the new data warehousing project codenamed "Trishul," he needed to submit a comprehensive project plan in just ten days.

Preparing a number of planning documents was daunting for Gokul. Despite the diligence of Gokul's core team, many documents were incomplete. Further, the list of required plans seemed endless: milestone list, high-level budget, human resource requirements, communication and risk management plans, and so on. Dependencies between plans made the task even more challenging.

The team felt overburdened as much of the information they needed was not available. They realized that too much guesswork and too many assumptions would put the project at risk. They were stalled.

"I'm not going to let this situation control me," Gokul told himself in a determined voice. He called his mentor Elva, a Program Director who had worked with the company for 11 years.

Elva patiently listened to Gokul's problems. She had been through similar situations and felt that all Gokul needed was proper guidance.

She spoke reassuringly: "Don't be too hard on yourself Gokul! I've faced tougher problems at project start. Break down the work. Tackle one document at a time. I've seen you get through worse situations before. Let me share a secret that'll get you out of this rut..."

Elva's genuine encouragement lifted Gokul's spirits. "Tell me, Elva," he eagerly said.

The mentor continued, "Fortunately for us, our company has developed high levels of project management maturity. Detailed records from past projects are available in our KnowStar knowledge base. All project managers have access to it.

"KnowStar stores valuable info on all projects completed in the past six years: Scope, Schedule, and Cost Baselines. Detailed data of planned and actual costs for work packages, work breakdown structures, risk registers and quality checklists. Most importantly, the database also has information on mistakes made in past projects and best practices that helped them."

Gokul was visibly relieved. He asked, "Can I search for info specific to data warehousing projects?".

Elva explained: "Of course, Gokul. The database is fully keyword searchable. Except for classified projects, you can access planning documents for all others. Much of the info you want is already available.

"But don't rely totally on past project data. Carry out sanity checks and make necessary adjustments.

"Don't forget how valuable this data was for you. When you complete your project, make sure you upload detailed data into the database."

His amazing knowledge repository of past projects is putting today's pieces together at warp speed!!

Elva added that such a database didn't exist when she started as a project manager. She was able to get tons of valuable information from team members who had worked on similar projects. She also ensured that the data on all her projects were collated and securely stored.

She had championed the need for building a comprehensive project knowledge database by building on her own success stories and those of other managers. That was how KnowStar was born.

Gokul felt a huge load lifted off his shoulders. He purposefully strode to his desk to start accessing KnowStar.

He was now confident of completing his detailed project plans well in time.

⊛ EXPERT INSIGHTS

Fahad Ahmed PMP, ITIL

RVP – Project Manager, Enterprise Project Management Department, Faysal Bank.

Projects in Canada, Pakistan, USA. **Industries:** Business Process Outsourcing, Financial Services, Insurance.

14+ years of experience in ERP, SDLC, strategy development and implementation, business analysis, risk management, setting up PMOs, delivery, governance, and change management. President PMI Karachi Chapter, PMI volunteer, graduate of PMI's Leadership Institute Master Class 2017.

Frequent research has outlined the benefits of having past data contributing to projects and project management success for any organization.

It is critical for organizations of any size to document lessons learned and use these wisely in such cases where project information is minimum at the start. Documenting project success stories can have a huge impact on any organization's project management maturity and definitely result in continuous improvement. Besides increasing project success rates, these factors also enhance organizational reputation.

Leveraging data from past projects will ensure (a) effective decision-making; (b) efficient resource usage; and (c) lessen individual dependency.

Sukumar Rajagopal B.E. (HONS.) EEE, IOD Certified Director, Tiny Habits Certified Coach

Founder & CEO, Tiny Magiq.

Projects in France, India, Norway, Philippines, UAE, UK, USA and many other countries through the global delivery model. **Industries:** Entertainment, Healthcare, Logistics, Manufacturing, Media, Retail.

29+ years of experience in program management, innovation, knowledge management, change management, and IT strategy.

With 100,000+ people and thousands of projects being executed, this was a big problem. The searchable project database we set up had become unusable due to too many search results. A key leader in my team proposed an excellent idea. Since we follow a well-defined process and a project management plan, she suggested that we deliver the relevant artifacts (guidance, knowledge, templates, etc.) right into the context of the project. Project execution significantly improved.

But could we find relevant case studies for business development? We set up a forum that helped get answers from experts with an SLA of four hours. For free form knowledge, we rolled out a blogging system. This system proved surprisingly popular and helped spread several innovative ideas virally through the organization.

Vadim Bogdanov PMP, PfMP, CFA

Founder, Bogdanov Associates, PM Advisory and Consultancy firm.

Projects in Australia, Belarus, Cyprus, Estonia, Kazakhstan, Latvia, Lithuania, Moldova, Germany, Romania, Russia, UK, Ukraine, USA. **Industries:** Banking and Finance, Civil Engineering, Engineering, Government, Information Technology, Manufacturing, Oil and Gas, Telecommunications.

17+ years creating PMOs, governance, and project management frameworks.

Author, Consultant, Trainer, Board Member. Authored four books on project management, designed numerous training programs, and founded Russia's first PM advisory and consulting firm.

I am often placed in situations where I have to select a project manager for a project. I use a simple trick to find the best candidate. I ask them to present, based on their experience:

- *Who were the typical stakeholders in your project?*
- *What are the risks you typically encounter?*
- *What does a typical WBS look like?*
- *Examples of how you arrived at time and cost estimates.*

Candidates who can confidently answer these questions demonstrate their true professionalism, expertise in specific project types and commitment for self-improvement. They also show that they can analyze lessons learned from past projects. I typically find that only one candidate in ten has these qualities. Using this approach, you will not only know how to start your project but also stand out from the crowd.

KEYS TO SUCCESS

- Start a project well, and you are well on your way to success.

- Perform a pre-mortem analysis to understand high risks.

- Do not succumb to the seductive appeal of customers and leaders to rush into execution. Rather, question them to understand the real objectives.

- You can ease your planning tasks by accessing relevant data from project knowledge bases. Else, you will be overwhelmed by the sheer volume of planning work involved at the early stages of the project.

- If your organization doesn't have a comprehensive repository, you can get a wealth of information from your project team members or colleagues who have experience in similar projects.

- When you complete a project, make sure you document data from your project in a systematic manner. These archives will help you in planning for future projects.

18 Zero Sum Game or Not?

Thiago was assigned a high-visibility project leading a 200-member team. The project involved archiving 26-year legacy data for a Texas-based law firm. Around 75 law graduates had been hired on a nine-month contract to help with summarizing and indexing digital documents. An immediate requirement was to procure 100 laptops for use by the team members. The cost of these laptops had already been built into the project budget.

Thiago called for bids from several firms selling computers and peripherals. He shortlisted two companies for a final decision. Aztec quoted $800 per laptop with a one-year on-site warranty. IntellectIT offered it at $960 per laptop with three years' comprehensive warranty. To make a fair comparison, Thiago added a 25% per year warranty cost to Aztec's price. Each laptop would now cost $1200.

He realized that IntellectIT's offer would save the company $24,000 in the long run. However, his project duration was only ten months. Aztec's proposal would save Thiago's project $16,000. Why would he want to pay second and third-year warranty on laptops that he wouldn't require after a year?

Thiago faced the dilemma every project manager contends with in a project of this type: Should he put his project first or organization first? If he carefully controlled project expenses and executed well, he would step up one level in the organization. Buying from IntellectIT would save the company $24,000 on warranty costs. But then, Thiago's project would have to absorb the extra $160 per laptop.

Faced with a difficult decision, he requested a solution from his manager, Harpreet Kaur. After hearing what Thiago had to say, Harpreet stated that there were no easy solutions. She asked Thiago to come up with an ideal solution.

Disappointed that he hadn't received any solid advice, Thiago went on a long drive, thinking of what best he could do. On Monday morning, he met Harpreet with his solution. He would take IntellectIT's offer, saving the organization $24,000.

He requested Harpreet to mention to top management that adding $16,000 to his project cost was saving the organization $24,000. "I would rather take a helicopter view than a Harley Davidson view," he told Harpreet, therefore making it clear that he was putting organizational interests above his own.

He also made a plea requesting her to approve an adjustment to reduce the extra cost from his project's profitability calculations. This way, his project would not suffer from lower profitability for a decision taken for organizational benefit.

The boss agreed. Armed with this confidence at the start of the project, Thiago was able to make several such win-win decisions throughout the project.

Harpreet could see that Thiago, unlike other project managers, did not have blinkers on, looking out only for his project's interests. He possessed the ability to see the big picture and was already thinking and communicating beyond his title.

She made up her mind to recommend a promotion for Thiago in that year's appraisal.

EXPERT INSIGHTS

Joanna Newman MBA, MCMI, PMP

Portfolio Manager, Vodafone, Canada.

Projects in Australia, Korea, UK, USA. **Industries:** Media, Research and Development, Telecommunications.

15+ years in project management for top technology companies. PMI UK Chapter Board volunteer since 2012.

Successful project managers focus on the "win triangle" when solving issues. The three points of the win triangle are:

- *The right solution for your project*
- *The right solution for your organization*
- *The solution which is beneficial to your reputation*

An example would be when one supplier is cheaper than the other, though their post sales support is weaker. Some might focus on the savings to the project only, ignoring the fact that the total cost to the organization is higher. Some might prefer the best supplier, even if they purchase support contracts they don't need. The win triangle will help you identify the best solution for your project and your organization, which in turn will benefit your reputation and your career.

Kwame Justice B.Ats, CPMgt, CNMP

Founder and Executive Chairman at Justice Societies, International NGO specialized in mentoring and empowerment.

Projects in Ghana, Ukraine, USA. **Industries:** Construction, Entertainment, Finance, Insurance, Media, NGOs.

11+ years of deep expertise in policy-making and development. Volunteer with the PMI Ghana Chapter (2016-2017).

Difficult dilemmas and conflicts are very common in global teams with age-diverse workforces, different values, and dissimilar work ethics. To achieve success, you will need to quickly take these challenges head on and resolve them effectively.

Among the toughest dilemmas are those that involve conflicts of interest where what is right for the organization is not necessarily good for the individual. Ethical and professional behavior demands that you accord higher priority to organizational interests. However, that does mean that you become a sacrificial lamb.

Innovative win-win solutions can be found using careful analysis, open communication, and collaboration involving all stakeholders from the oldest veterans to the youngest team members. Adopting this approach, I was able to successfully implement a global initiative while leading a multigenerational team from three continents.

KEYS TO SUCCESS

- As a project manager, you often face dilemmas in balancing organizational and personal goals. It is tough to take such decisions when your career could be harmed.
- Choose conscience over comfort. Ethical and professional conduct requires you to pick options that benefit the organization over those that benefit your project.
- Choosing the easy option of benefiting your project can hurt career growth since it creates the image that you can't think beyond your project.
- By thinking innovatively, you can devise win-win solutions.
- Effectively communicate these solutions to management to demonstrate your ability to think beyond your project.
- This approach is valuable in achieving career growth.

Scoping the 5 Cs

Energized by strong coffee and delicious cookies, participants of the "Scope It with Success" workshop were geared up for the post-tea session.

Klaus, the workshop facilitator, remarked: "Many important research studies confirm that over 70% of projects suffer from serious scope management issues. Today, we'll cover the five Cs required for effective scope management. But to begin with, what are your biggest scope management challenges?"

Attendees began to voice their viewpoints.

"We had already listed down many requirements before we went to customers."

"Clients don't know what they want."

"Ambiguity!"

"Customers try to add requirements that have no link to the business case."

"Clients are like Oliver Twist, always wanting more!" said Mikhail, making everyone laugh.

Klaus asked the participants to pause. He said, "Hold on, folks! Let's look for solutions to these challenges.

"Group activity time. We'll consider four major areas: Stakeholder Involvement, Understanding Expectations, Agile Methods, Effective Tools. Please assemble into four groups so that we can discuss specific solutions in these areas."

He started a countdown clock, setting it to 20 minutes. Rotating among the groups, he offered expert suggestions.

Klaus then announced: "Six minutes to go. Time to pick a team spokesperson who'll summarize your proposed solutions!"

As the clock wound down to zero, he said: "Time's up. Which team wants to go first?"

Mano went first. "Our team discussed stakeholder engagement. We had many great ideas. It helps to involve stakeholders early, frequently, and in-depth. Walt suggested that teams start with top honchos and understand their big picture needs. We then talk to the next level of executives in the client organization and go on to the last level of users. Mikhail likened this to the WBS approach. It helps to collect requirements with a top-down approach."

Max summarized next, starting by thanking his team for their valuable suggestions. Francois had opined that it was commonplace for team members to focus too much on technical aspects of requirements. Since understanding customer business requirements was critical, his team ensured that they included a few business analysts in every session. Kate had mentioned the remarkable value added by a team member who was a certified PMI-PBA® (Professional in Business Analysis).

Klaus was impressed. He said, "Those are great points. Let's hear from the other two groups."

Ashraf's group had discussed agile techniques. He said, "Many in our group have worked as Scrum masters or as contributors to agile projects. We stressed that it is not enough to engage stakeholders only in the early stages. Continuous collaboration is critical in clarifying requirements.

"Lucio made an excellent point about how writing requirements in the form of user stories make them easy to understand. Mingyu said that many a time, customers were unable to articulate their needs. She spoke about how her team used simple diagrams to give customers a visual feel of the final deliverables. Often, she was able to make early design fixes based on user feedback."

"I don't know what I want but I know what I don't want"

Cindy spoke next. "Thank God, we are last!" She smiled. "I got a few extra few minutes to summarize all the excellent ideas my team came up with!

"There are so many valuable tools for PMs to leverage. We discussed context diagrams, dataflow diagrams, mind mapping tools and much more. When Victor suggested Ishikawa diagrams, we were, at first, perplexed. He showed us how fishbone diagrams are a valuable tool in many areas, not just quality. Awesome free versions of these tools are available online.

"I could go on and on, but will stop since our time is up."

"Wow! These are all brilliant points. What were the five C's we spoke about? Continuous Customer Collaboration, Clarity, and Comprehensiveness of Scope.

"We are all benefiting from the collective wisdom! We've had much food for thought today. We'll do a deeper dive tomorrow. See you bright and early at nine!"

EXPERT INSIGHTS

Ravi Vurakaranam PMP

Director, Cognizant Technology Solutions, India.

Projects in India, UK, USA. **Industries:** Entertainment, Information Technology, Life Sciences, Media.

26+ years. Deep expertise in effective PMOs. Volunteer with PMI since 2005. Currently President of the PMI Hyderabad Chapter. Was earlier employed in a steel manufacturing unit as a project engineer in the construction of integrated steel plants in India and abroad.

Scope clarity is a major project success factor. These are critical lessons I learned in my experience across several projects:

- *Often, customers cannot visualize the end product. If you assume the opposite, your project journey is likely to be bumpy.*
- *Work on detailed project requirements, adopting an iterative approach where necessary.*
- *When you face technical challenges, use the proof of concept approach to substantiate our assumptions.*
- *Strengthen your requirement-gathering process by engaging experienced business analysts in documenting requirements.*
- *Detailed acceptance criteria are invaluable in clarifying requirements.*
- *Completing requirements before contract finalization is an effective step in reducing project risk.*

John Watson PMP, PMI-ACP

Entrepreneur and Consultant, USA.

Projects in the USA. **Industries:** Communications, Education, Finance, Human Resources, Healthcare, Information Technology, Logistics.

Senior leadership positions with major telecommunications clients. Operations and project/program management.

Let's be clear about clarity!

Defining and achieving clarity is your number one and most important requirement.

Remember Stephen Covey's habit #2, Begin with the End in Mind: "Begin each task or project with a clear vision of your direction and destination."

Be clear about your roles, responsibilities, and the expectations of who does what, when, and why.

Be clear about what success and completion look like.

Do not rush to the how. Be patient as that will become more clear the closer you get to completion!

Your assumptions are not always the assumptions of others.

KEYS TO SUCCESS

- Fuzzy scope, unclear requirements, and scope creep seriously affect over 70% of projects.
- Effective scope management helps you substantially increase the probability of project success.
- Involve stakeholders, especially clients, early in the project. By doing this, you can save considerable time.
- Use a top-down approach. Start by understanding big picture expectations of major stakeholders. Collect from the next level of users and continue till all user levels are covered.
- Leverage the capabilities of business analysts who can be invaluable in helping translate customer requirements.
- Employ tools such as context diagrams, data flow diagrams, mind mapping tools, and fishbone diagrams to improve the requirements collection process.
- Leverage agile techniques such as frequent customer collaboration, user stories, and phased delivery.

Where Did That Come From? 20

There was palpable energy on day two of the "Scope It with Success" workshop. Buoyed by Klaus's engaging and problem-solving approach on day one, participants were eager to learn more.

After summarizing the previous day's discussions, the facilitator said, "Let's look at the issues that remain."

He scored off the topics the four groups had already covered. He listed what remained:

- Clients are like Oliver Twist, always wanting more!
- Customers try to add requirements that have no link to the business case.

Klaus continued: "Both relate to demanding customers. Anyone here had a client who didn't want more?"

Sumit, a quiet participant so far, raised his hand.

"Wow, Sumit! You're truly blessed! Is your project hiring? I'm sure we'd all like to join!" Klaus joked, as everyone laughed.

The facilitator then asked for a show of hands of those who had heard about the Requirements Traceability Matrix (RTM). Around two-thirds indicated that they were familiar with the term.

Klaus next asked, "How many of you have used the technique?"

Addressing the handful of attendees who had, he asked, "In what ways can RTM help control scope?"

Francois responded immediately. "RTMs we use in our projects include a column on how every requirement connects to a business need, opportunity, goal, or project objective."

"Each time a customer mentions a requirement, our business analysts ask them how this need will satisfy project goals. If a connection can't be made, it is probably an unmet need from a previous project."

Mingyu excitedly responded. "Perfect situation where agile MoSCoW[1] fits in!" She added that requirements with a strong connect to overall business goals were put in the "Must Have" and "Should Have" categories. Those with weak or no connections would go into the "Could Have" or "Won't Have" categories.

Mano too chimed in. "Customers are so demanding that we often end up with very long lists of requirements. Invariably, time and cost constraints create a situation where many requirements will need to be dropped from scope statements. Perhaps, we can have a 5-point rating scale of the connection between a requirement and project goals. This score can help ease the usually tough task of prioritization!"

Klaus complimented the participants for their input. He added, "I've often helped clients leverage the RTM in another way. Do we have the time before lunch to discuss this?"

---

[1] https://en.wikipedia.org/wiki/MoSCoW_method

"10 minutes," quipped someone.

"Far more than I need," Klaus said, continuing, "I ask PMOs to add a 'Requester' column to their RTMs. Teams are trained to make sure that this column is filled in for every requirement.

These crumbs are priceless!!!!! they help us trace back, saving time and money!

"This info is invaluable during design when our teams need specific clarifications. They now know the best person to clarify their doubts. In the worst case that the requester has left the client organization, we still know which team or department can provide clarifications.

"Writing down requester info is a simple, painless step during requirement gathering. But let me assure you, it will save you a lot of pain, time, and therefore money!"

The attendees had carefully jotted down notes as Klaus spoke. Loaded with food for thought, the group broke for lunch.

EXPERT INSIGHTS

Thomas George PMP, PMI-RMP, MSP, CC

Director of Consulting Services at one of the largest Canadian Information Technology companies.

Projects in Canada, USA. **Industries:** Lottery and Gaming, Utilities.

Excellent track record of delivering high-profile and complex projects. Several volunteer positions with PMI, the latest being VP – Communications for the PMI New Brunswick Chapter.

The Requirement Traceability Matrix (RTM) is a powerful tool a project manager should use to manage scope. This is especially true for projects that are ambiguous. Having a clear requirements document and the RTM will help ensure the project is set up for success. Here are some of the benefits I have personally realized by using RTMs.

- *Helps identify issues during the early stages of the project, which is less expensive compared to later project phases.*
- *Ensures that no requirements are missed as we move from one project phase to another.*
- *Maps the requirements to the project goal, thereby ensuring that we are focusing on the right scope.*
- *Sets expectation with all stakeholders up front, thus avoiding disappointment during the later stages of the project.*

Zahara Khan PMP

Head of Operations, Aga Khan Social Welfare Board for Pakistan.

Projects in Pakistan, USA. **Industries**: Education, Healthcare, Information Technology, Social Development.

An award-winning leader with a passion for international development and professional excellence. 22+ years' experience leading award-winning and internationally acknowledged multi sectoral programs. Co-founder of two social enterprises. Volunteer with PMI since 2007. President of PMI Karachi Chapter (2013–14). Member of PMI Ethics Appeals Committee (2016) and Member of PMI Ethics Member Advisory Group.

In a recent time-critical project, we were facing recurring issues of "gold plating" as the junior project manager was facing challenges controlling the scope creep.

We took the decision to break our project requirements into smaller work packages and prioritized each in consultation with the client, and documented the priorities in an RTM. We also used this prioritized list to develop a consensus on the timelines for delivery of each work package.

This whole process greatly helped with clear communication among all stakeholders, controlling scope creep, and delivering the project on time.

KEYS TO SUCCESS

- Know your customer. Demanding customers are the norm in modern projects.
- Stop the flow of never-ending requirements. You would have seen that in many industries, time and cost constraints severely limit the requirements that can be fitted into the project scope statement.
- Often, requirements left over from a past project may be moved to a succeeding project. Be ready to descope your project.
- The Requirement Traceability Matrix (RTM) is an invaluable tool which you can leverage. As your team gathers requirements, instruct them to collect this info:
  - ➤ Business need, opportunity, goal, or project objective. This information is extremely useful in prioritization.
  - ➤ Requester. This information will be invaluable when you require clarifications on requirements. Your team will know the right people to contact.
- Follow the above steps to save significant cost and time.
- You can employ the well-known MoSCoW technique in your projects to prioritize requirements.

21 A Risky Proposition

It was a late evening in the conference room on the 11th floor of the city hotel. A workshop titled "Practical Risk Management for Project Success" was on. However, there was no risk of participants dozing off since Kumar, the facilitator, was as energetic and passionate as he was in the morning.

Loud beeps of a fire alarm sounded as he moved to a new slide.

Kumar dramatically said, "Imagine the lights just went off. The fire alarm sounds. Sprinklers come on. You can smell chemicals in the air.

"We all know you need to reach the fire exits, but do you know where they are? Can you reach them in pitch darkness? What will you do? Are you panicking? I bet you are.

"A similar situation happens when a major project risk event has just occurred. The customer is agitated. Your boss is livid. He demands immediate answers. You gather a team of subject matter experts and head into your project war room. What kind of solution will you come up with when the sword of Damocles seems to hang over your head? Can you make the right decisions in a state of panic?

"It's almost end of the day, but let's have a show of hands. How many of you have been in this situation before?"

Attendees raised their hands.

Kumar continued. "Let's assume that you've moved locations. You're working late on the 5th floor of your office. You've worked there for over two years. The fire alarm sounds, with the same sprinkler and chemical smell situation. Will you panic now?

"I suppose not. You've been through fire drills several times and knew exactly where the staircases are. You also know the safe zones you need to assemble in.

"Let's move to projects. A major risk event has caused your customer to be distraught, and your boss is furious. He immediately needs to know what you plan to do.

"You suppress a smile. Having carried out practical risk management early in your project, you know there are three viable risk response options. You tell your boss, 'We thought about this before. Give me 15 minutes. I will consult with my team and let you know which of Plan A, B, or C will best remedy this situation!'

"You present the picture of a confident, professional project manager. Gathering your team in the war room, you analyze which of the response plans best suits this situation. There is no panic since the response plans were devised early in the project when the team had the luxury of clear thinking. Your boss is impressed!"

Kumar added that the value of practical risk management is well known. However, severe constraints force project managers to adopt a mechanical approach to project risk management. Many just "go through the motions," filling out forms and templates to ensure a tick mark on a project audit.

He added that his consulting experience proved that it was critical to keep project risk management processes practical.

Kumar explained: "Adopt a simple, practical approach to project risks. Make risk identification fun. Aim to gather as many risks as possible. Work with your team to analyze the risks to come up with a short list of high-priority risks.

"I believe that effective risk management can be one of the best contributors to project success. However, sadly, it is one of most neglected areas.

"If you don't carry out effective risk management, you are taking on significant risks!

"Bandwidth is indeed a big constraint. But you don't have to go for an all-or-nothing approach. Start small. Notch up quick wins. Build on the confidence of these quick wins to achieve bigger victories. Believe me. I've done it, and you can too!"

Kumar's passion and his energetic words seemed to have a carry-over effect. The participants said in chorus to Kumar, "Consider it done."

⬡ EXPERT INSIGHTS

Milton A Carvajal MSCIS, PMP

IT Project Manager at Miami Children's Health System.

Projects in China, India, USA. **Industries:** Airlines, Healthcare, Hospitality.

15+ years in Information Technology including waterfall and agile methodologies. Graduate of the PMI Leadership Institute Master Class 2012. Toastmaster Competent Communicator. Private Pilot.

Project managers face intense pressure to get the project done on time, within budget and scope. Done right, risk management significantly reduces this stress. Very early in my career, I was fortunate to learn the many advantages of effective project risk management. That experience was a real game changer.

A great best practice is to engage the team early, starting with the project charter. Discuss risk management in all your subsequent meetings. When identifying risk, start meetings with risk examples to get team members involved in the process. Make sure you take good notes and start thinking of who will own these risks. Using a risk template with the following columns was extremely useful: Risk Id. Author. Date registered. Risk Category. Description of Risk. Risk Owner. Probability. Impact. Risk Score. Proximity/Urgency. Contingency. Risk Status.

Zulkhernain Shamsuddin, PhD, GPM, ITIL (Expert), CPRM, CITP, Certified Trainer - American Academy of Project Management, Certified Projects Director

Senior IT Risk Management Consultant, Zulk Consulting Pte Ltd.

Projects in Indonesia, Malaysia, Singapore, Thailand. **Industries**: Banking and Financial Services, Consultancy, Education, Information Technology.

27 years in evaluating and implementing project and risk management processes and methodologies. Deep expertise in information technology projects including commercial off-the-shelf applications.

Some projects use no approach whatsoever to risk management. They are either ignorant, running their first project, or they are somehow confident that no risks will occur in their project.

I'm speechless! Is this for real? If you do not truly embed risk management in your project, you will not be able to deliver the committed project objectives, and the likelihood of your project failing is high. Try making risk management part of the Key Performance Indicators (KPI) of your project.

KEYS TO SUCCESS

- Effective risk management can be one of the biggest contributors to increasing the probability of project success.
- Make sure your team avoids a templated approach to risk management, even when constrained by limited bandwidth.
- Do not fall prey to the temptation of merely passing the project audit. Instead, make your risk management practical and useful.
- Plan how you will carry out risk management. Identify a significant number of risks.
- Filter for the most important risks by considering the probability and impact of each risk.
- Plan risk responses for the short-listed risks.
- Periodically, review your risk register for new risks, risks that went away and those that might have changed in probability or impact. Plan risk responses for new risks.

Explicitly Excluded

"**W**onderful Wednesday, Mike," several team members greeted Mike cheerily as he walked in. They were rather surprised to hear an unusually low-voiced "Morning everyone." His colleagues wondered what was wrong. After all, the project was progressing remarkably well!

The project manager slumped into his plush leather chair in his cabin, presumably perplexed. Most team members did not know about the previous day's conference call that had caused Mike considerable worry. In that call, the customer had demanded extra work which involved an additional effort of 400 hours. Mike could not flatly refuse. The change request meant inflated costs with no additional payment. Worse, it would drive his project hopelessly behind schedule. He remembered reading a PMI "Pulse of the Profession® In Depth Report" on Requirements Management which said, "When counting the number of causes of project failure, you need more than one hand. But the leading culprits will always include scope creep, poor communication, lack of stakeholder involvement…"

"So, which MVP do you want? Minimally Viable Product
or Maximally Volatile Product?"

As Mike mulled over the available options, Kripa, one of the project's module leaders, knocked on the cabin door. She had come in for a scheduled weekly meeting. Noticing his worried look, she asked, "What's up, Mike?"

"You were there in the customer call last evening. Didn't the demand for additional functionality worry you? It will kill both our schedule and our budget!"

Kripa smiled. "Yes. Accepting those demands will cause us a lot of damage. But there's a way out of this potential mess!"

Mike was intrigued. The project lead continued, "Remember the Project Success workshop you arranged for my fellow project leads and me? One of the essential techniques we learned was to include a detailed list of explicitly excluded requirements.

The scope statement our customer signed off on includes over 200 such items. Please open the document."

Mike's face lit up as he read through the scope statement. The "Explicit Exclusions" section included the functionality now being demanded by the client. "Awesome work, Kripa! The team's efforts in compiling this list will save the day!"

The client accepted Mike's urgent request for an afternoon meeting. Before the meeting, Kripa emailed the client representative, explaining the Explicit Exclusions section signed by them. She gently pointed out that the delays and the increased cost that the added functionality would cause.

During the call, the customer's representative said, "You have a point. We should have thought about this earlier. However, this is a critical requirement. We just can't do without this functionality! Can you please suggest a solution?"

Mike told the customer representative that his team has already worked out the additional cost and time. The new requirement would add $20,000 to the budget and would require a seven-week schedule extension. A brief round of negotiations followed, and finally, the two sides agreed to an extra payment of $17,500 and six weeks of additional time.

Mike gave Kripa an instant appreciation letter, specifying her timely contribution after the meeting ended. He made a mental note to immediately approve his project leaders' requests to attend the next set of Project Success workshops.

⬡ EXPERT INSIGHTS

Esteban Villegas PMP

Regional Program Manager, McCain Foods, Colombia.

Projects in Argentina, Brazil, Chile, Colombia, Ecuador, Mexico, Perú, Venezuela. **Industries:** Food and Beverages, Finance, Information Technology, Insurance, Manufacturing, Telecommunications.

14+ years of project management experience, with deep expertise in multi-country projects and PMOs. Global PMI volunteer since 2008.

Do you document detailed "out of scope" elements while obtaining project approvals? This technique is critical for all projects, especially when you are providing consultancy in outsourced project management services.

Overlooking specific exclusions often happens in the process of finalizing project scope sign-offs.

The solution? Use a detailed "out of scope" section which includes a thorough list of the items not included in your project's deliverables. Time and cost savings can be achieved through reduced discussions and fewer misunderstandings. Change requests are also handled more efficiently.

The resultant savings are invaluable in delivering successful projects.

Sriram Srinivasan MBA, PMP, ITIL Expert, CISA, CISM, CGEIT, CRISC, CBCI, AMBCI, TOGAF, LA ISO 20000, 27001 and 22301.

Principal Consultant, GRC Projects, Dubai.

Projects in India, Qatar, Saudi Arabia, UAE, USA. **Industries:** Banking, Education, Finance, Government, Information Technology, Insurance, Oil and Gas, Telecommunication.

17+ years of professional experience in project, program management, and management consulting. Proven track record in managing projects in the areas of ITSM, information security, business continuity, aligning with regulations, governance, risk, and compliance. PMI volunteer, trainer and expert contributor to PMI's PMBOK® Guide 5 and 6 (Draft Review Contribution).

Project success demands constant, effective management of scope, time, and cost baselines. I achieved excellent results by leveraging the powerful DDA Technique:

Documentation: *Involve all key project stakeholders, carefully recording their requirements. Ensure that these are well-documented in the scope statement.*

Demarcation: *Clearly segregate scope inclusions and exclusions. Make sure both categories are very exhaustive.*

Agreement: *Proactively discuss and where required, negotiate with all relevant parties. Spare no effort to reach clear agreements. Pay particular attention to explicit scope exclusions.*

The results? Minimized scope creep, reduction in disputes and project success.

KEYS TO SUCCESS

- By avoiding scope creep, you can significantly increase chances of project success.
- As a project manager, you often guide your teams through detailed scope discussion.
- During these discussions and those involving time and cost estimates, your team members often note down scope exclusions. You may not usually document these exclusions in the project statement. However, your clients may still believe these are in scope.
- Guide your teams to explicitly document all exclusions in a separate section of the scope statement.
- In reviewing the scope statement, your customers may insist that these items be included.
- Win-win negotiations can help clarify the scope and prevent late-stage disagreements.

23   Two Wins in a Row

"OK, Joe. I'll do my best," Thiago said, as he finished the call with his company's CEO. He looked visibly anxious. His boss had asked him to head the negotiation team to finalize the terms for a major logistics automation order for Yummybites Foods, a mid-sized company.

Thiago had worked with ValueWorks Solutions for close to two years. Though he had managed several customer negotiations, the sheer size of this order unnerved him. The results of the negotiations could make or break his career. Realizing that he needed expert help, he called up his mentor Ammarah, an experienced project manager who worked elsewhere.

Ammarah was ready with her seasoned advice: "Not all negotiations are the same. To ensure a mutually satisfying outcome, you should apply the key components of successful negotiations recommended by William Ury, co-founder of the Program on Negotiation at Harvard University." She highlighted three key points:

a. *Generate efficiency. Successful negotiations require you to accord high priority to honing your negotiation skills. Detailed planning is the first step. Understand the key priorities for your project and those of the other party. Determine the price point or other limits at which you will be forced to walk away.*

b. *Strive for win-win. As Dr. Stephen Covey rightly says, "In the long run, if it is a win for only one of us, we both lose. Win-win is the only real alternative in most situations."*

c. *Maintain or enhance relationships between the negotiating parties. Your aim should be to extract the best possible deal without damaging the relationship.*

On the bright and sunny day of the meeting, Thiago was initially surprised to see that Yummybites had brought along two very experienced negotiators.

Hey! You can play the counting game on the iPad!

Now that's what I call a real win-win deal!

Wow! I love iPad games!

Win-win negotiations before the math exam!

The customers demanded that the project be completed within a budget of $5.8 million. Thiago countered with a budget of $7.2 million. His boss had told him to accept nothing lower than $6.5 million.

Arguments and counterarguments followed. Yummybites' representatives finally offered $6.7 million. ValueWorks' Marketing Manager Richard Summers bluntly said the offer was much below par, having noticed one of the Yummybites representatives pulling at his collar, fidgeting and displaying signs of desperation. Richard was sure he could push them to go much higher.

Thiago had two choices: Continue to play hardball, not bothering about the negative consequences to the relationship. Or, reach a compromise where both parties would win. He mentally chose the latter. Requesting a brief break, he met with his three colleagues in another room.

"Let's not drive them too hard. Let's compromise so that we can win this deal and build a long-term relationship. We are, after all, getting more than what we would have originally settled for."

Back at the meeting, he told the Yummybites representatives that he would accept the deal provided a small piece of work worth $50,000 was dropped from the scope. Based on his homework, he knew that this scope was not high on the customer's priority list.

The clients objected at first but finally relented. Soon after the working lunch, the contract was signed.

Thiago's boss was elated. The whole team celebrated that evening at Italian Delights, a highly-rated restaurant.

EXPERT INSIGHTS

Acilio Marinello PMP, CSPO, PMO-CC

Deliver Thinker, Practical Thinking Group.

Projects in Brazil, Lebanon, UAE, USA. **Industries:** Consulting, Finance, Telecom.

16+ years. Deep expertise in global projects. PMI volunteer since 2010. Finance Director PMI São Paulo Chapter (2013–14) and Member of PMIef Engagement Committee (2015–16).

Negotiation should be one of the most important skills in a project manager's toolkit. This skill is especially critical in global projects.

Global projects add these unique challenges and complexities:

- *Team members located in different countries.*
- *Different cultures, beliefs, and habits.*
- *Lack of personal and frequent contact between team members.*

In this context, negotiating agreements with the win-win approach becomes vital in order to expedite the project, encourage greater autonomy for team members, and solidify trust among stakeholders.

Barbara Porter MBA, PMP, SaFE, SCM, SSGB

Chief Technology Officer of Fragrance.com.

Projects in Australia, Brazil, Canada, Costa Rica, India, UK, USA. **Industries:** Consumer Goods, Gifting Services, Information Technology, Internet, Petroleum, Retail.

Nearly 20 years working for internet retailers specializing in software development, project management, data science, and operational efficiency and agility.

Many people think about negotiations in terms of a freshly baked pie. Some people go into negotiations trying to get all of it. Others try to get to an even 50/50 split.

Knowing what is important to the party you are negotiating with is essential to creating a win/win situation, the ideal outcome of any negotiation. Maybe one party loves the fruit filling, while the other loves the crust. Maybe one party wants all the whipped cream on top, and the other party doesn't want whipped cream at all. What if one party wants the pie plate more than the pie itself? These are all opportunities to define at and split up the "pie" differently.

Now, what if you're willing to give the other party the recipe used to make the pie? Look for opportunities to give things that don't "cost" you much and maybe the other party will give you more parts of the pie that you care about!

KEYS TO SUCCESS

- As a project manager, you are involved in a number of negotiations with various stakeholders.
- In many negotiations, you may approach a "winner takes all approach" to get the best possible deal for your organization. However, this approach may rarely be successful in the long term.
- Win-win negotiations are more sustainable.
- To excel at such negotiations, you need to invest time in planning.
- Analyze the priorities of both parties to the negotiation.
- Some items may be of low-priority to the other party but higher on your priority list. Negotiating on these items gives you greater chances of success.

Paint the Big Picture

24

Naomi couldn't understand why Gokul would do something so unusual. She walked into Gokul's room and told him, "Why this meeting? It's a sheer waste of time! Many of the invitees don't even know what a WBS is. Between you and me, we know enough to get the job done in just two hours!"

Gokul headed a project to develop an Expense Management software solution for Keystone Associates, an engineering services firm.

Naomi, the project's assistant project manager, couldn't fathom why Gokul had just sent a meeting invite to twenty key members of the project team. Gokul wanted it to be a team activity to create the project's Work Breakdown Structure.

Gokul calmly responded by saying, "The meeting is certainly not a waste of time Naomi! My invite to all key team members has a definite purpose."

Naomi's doubts still remained.

Seeing Naomi's disapproving look, Gokul recalled a memorable town hall speech he had heard in a previous job. John, Senior VP of a global pharmaceutical company who addressed the gathering, had shown the photograph of a lady whose face was swollen beyond recognition due to a rare disease. Another snap taken 19 months later showed the smiling face of the same woman, almost completely cured by the company's medication.

John had stressed, "This is the difference your work makes to the lives of many people. Whether you are a system architect, DBA, Java developer, or tester you are ultimately making a meaningful difference to people's lives. Remember this when you come in for work every morning!"

The Vice President was driving home the point to the IT department that big picture visualization was most important. He had demonstrated that getting people to understand the larger purpose of their daily work would give them motivation of the highest order.

Gokul told Naomi that the meeting to build a WBS involving key team members would similarly help them understand the 30,000 feet view of the project.

This session would also confer the project with many additional benefits:

1. The ability to harness a larger pool of project experience and technical knowledge, resulting in a more comprehensive WBS.

2. When team members are invited to contribute to building the WBS, they feel respected for their expertise. Motivation levels of the project team are likely to soar.

3. Team members no longer feel a WBS was thrust on them, Buy-in on project requirements and scope is therefore much higher.

4. Being involved in the process gave them the confidence that this project's planning was systematic and thorough.

Gokul launched the meeting with a brief introduction to Work Breakdown Structures and how they helped the project. This introduction would help those who were new to the concept.

He added, "Naomi and I could have built the WBS ourselves. However, the wealth of experience in this room is going to make our WBS far better. Do share your experience and expertise. There will be prizes for the best suggestions."

The team got down to building the project's WBS and thoroughly enjoyed the experience. On completion, Gokul arranged for the document to be emailed to all the project team members.

He told the meeting participants, "Now, every team member can see the big picture of our project, not just you. Everyone can connect their tasks to the project's vision. They can clearly see how the bricks they're setting will add to the project's magnificent building!"

A year later, Naomi, now heading a project, asked Gokul, who had been promoted as senior PM, "Did you accept the meeting invite for the WBS building session?"

"Yes, I did," he said, with a knowing smile.

"Oh, that team is crazy about cricket!"

⬟ EXPERT INSIGHTS

Raju Rao B Tech, PMP, SCPM (Stanford Certified Project Manager)

Author, Speaker, and Social Entrepreneur.

Projects in India, UAE, USA. **Industries:** Construction, Engineering, Information Technology, Manufacturing, Telecommunications.

40+ years in engineering, project management, consulting and training, entrepreneurship. Member of the Standards Development Core team for PMI's OPM3 and PMI India's Leadership Team for Awards. Co-authored *Project Management Circa 2025*, a PMI publication, and *Organizational Project Management* published by Management Concepts. Speaker at PMI Global Congresses in Toronto, Bangkok, and Singapore. Speaker at several PMI chapter events in India and the USA.

Creating a WBS can be an exciting exercise when we use Post-it-notes. How does this help? We can leverage these while brainstorming and lateral thinking, and when we use top-down and bottom-up approaches. The ideal setting for this activity is a workshop situation with project participants fully involved in it.

Furthermore, the WBS can be used as a tool for varying purposes, e.g. scope, cost, resources, risk, estimation, etc. This can be done at different stages of the project life cycle. For this, the work package is used as a basic building block, and one can get multiple views by altering the purpose like building a Lego toy or solving a Rubik's cube puzzle.

Cristian Soto MPM, PMP

Consultant and Founder, Roleplay Consulting.

Projects in Brazil, Bolivia, Chile, Croatia, Paraguay, Peru, Spain. **Industries:** Education, Media, Telecommunications.

Passionate "questionologist," speaker, project management geek, edutech lover, and an avid discomfort zone seeker. Specializations: Project management, business simulation games, and experiential learning.

Paul works as PM in a fashion company. He heads a six-month project to develop a new, very elegant wristband.

Paul knows that the Work Breakdown Structure (WBS) is the key and prepares to conduct an effective WBS workshop. He actively engages with various senior functional managers in this workshop.

With a well-developed WBS, Paul starts work with his project team. However, very soon they realize that some critical deliverables need to be added to the original WBS. Having now understood the value of a detailed WBS, they regret having missed the WBS planning sessions. They resolve to attend these meetings in the future.

━━━ KEYS TO SUCCESS ━━━

- Effectively leverage Work Breakdown Structures to create buy-in among team members, and to build teamwork by motivating team members about the project's vision.

- Actively involve key members of your team in the process of building the project WBS. By doing so, you are demonstrating that you value their experience and expertise.

- Team involvement in building the WBS increases buy-in and morale.

- Circulate the WBS to other team members. They will now be able to connect their tasks to the big picture of the project.

- Using this approach, you can significantly increase morale and productivity.

25

RACIng to Clear Roles

On a cold Saturday afternoon, Mano's mind was fixated on the following week. She pulled on her sweater and began planning for the week ahead. Her top priority of the week was to assign tasks to project teams, something she felt challenged given the confusion and issues it had caused in past projects.

She remembered that neglect of some critical activities had resulted in significant delays in past projects. The root cause of the problems had been lack of clear task assignment.

"Oops! We didn't realize this was our team's responsibility!"

"Sorry! This task completely slipped my attention. Wasn't this assigned to Emilio?"

Task tracking turned a nightmare.

A year ago, Mano had learned about the value of RACI charts (also called Responsibility Assignment Matrices or RAM) in a three-day workshop. She had been using the technique in all her projects since then. But despite her efforts, complete role clarity remained elusive.

For the project in progress, she was in dire need of a new game plan. The project manager remembered connecting with Keith Chui, her former workshop trainer, through LinkedIn. Keith belonged to the rare breed of coaches who passionately advocated applying theory to generate solutions to problems in projects.

"No, it's not tic-tac-toe...but if you don't cross tasks off your list, you will get nought!"

Mano messaged Keith on LinkedIn, asking if he could help solve a problem. Keith responded with a yes. Mano sent an email detailing her challenges with RACI charts and requested a 30-minute Skype meeting for a discussion. In a couple of hours, Keith replied, allocating a slot for the very next day.

In the Skype call, Keith stated that while RACI charts were widely used, problems cropped up when their use was limited to either the project or team levels. Why? At the project level, roles and responsibilities of each team could remain unclear. At the team level, individual members lacked clarity.

Keith explained that an elegant solution would be to develop RACI charts at both the team and project levels. At the project level, rows would list work packages in the Work Breakdown Structure (WBS) with columns representing teams and cells showing team responsibilities. At the team level, rows would list tasks assigned to the team with columns representing individuals in the team.

He went on to say that using this approach teams, as well as individuals, would have role clarity. Further, the danger of tasks slipping between cracks would be minimized. Mano was delighted to learn this practical success secret and profusely thanked Keith for his timely advice.

Mano communicated the new approach to her team leaders on Monday. They were very appreciative of how this solution could solve the challenges of the past. They then prepared a Work Package level RACI chart with precise details of expectations from each team.

Using this chart as the input, each team leader then assigned team-level responsibilities to individual colleagues.

A couple of months later, Mano was relieved to learn that the elegant solution was working soundly. As a mark of gratitude, Mano wrote a glowing LinkedIn recommendation for Keith.

EXPERT INSIGHTS

Amany Nuseibeh MBT, PMP, CPPD, MSP Practitioner, P3O Practitioner

Project Management Consultant.

Projects around the globe, specifically Australia, UK, USA. **Industries:** Aviation, Construction & Property, Consulting, Education, Engineering & Maintenance, Finance, Information Technology, Manufacturing, Research, Resources & Mining, Services and Government, Telecommunications, Transport.

Volunteer, PMI Ethics Member Advisory Group. Past President, PMI Sydney Chapter.

15+ years of experience delivering complex, large-scale transformations, portfolios, programs, and projects in multiple industries.

As we prepare ourselves for a future that heavily utilizes virtual teams, digital technology, and increasingly flexible arrangements, it is imperative to provide the utmost clarity on the level of participation in each of the project's deliverables and tasks – that's where RACI comes to the rescue! Using the RACI matrix or any of its variations (examples include RASCI, RASIC where S = Supportive) is a good practice. Define it collaboratively with the project's team, giving them the opportunity to raise their hands and take ownership. Challenges arise when overlaps or gaps occur. Both need to be resolved to have each deliverable/task with one "R." Overlaps where a deliverable or task has more than one person responsible (more than one "R") will require further breaking-down to ensure responsibilities and commitments are obtained resulting in one "R." For gaps where there is no one responsible (no R), obtain a decision or a nomination from the person accountable or the approver on who would be the best to do the work. Confirm the team member's commitment, and assign the "R." Now that you've got the one who performs the work sorted-out, your job is much easier mapping the rest!

Prasannaa Sampathkumar PMP

Delivery Manager, DXC Technology.

Projects in France, Germany, India, Italy, Japan, Netherlands, Singapore, Sweden, UAE, UK, USA. **Industries:** Automobile, Manufacturing, and Insurance.

20+ years of IT technical and managerial experience in various domains. Volunteer with PMI for the past 10 years. Contributes in various volunteer leader positions. President of PMI Chennai Chapter (2016–18).

In today's volatile world, change is the only constant. When you experience a lot of changes in your team resources, RACI charts are the best way to ensure that people know their responsibilities. It also simplifies onboarding of new members. You can quickly explain what their responsibilities are in their specific roles, therefore eliminating confusion. I urge all my project managers to use RACI charts. I ensure that I review them as a part of every project review. Good RACI charts assure you of project success. They are among the most valuable project management tools. RACI charts are also extremely helpful in identifying poor performers who frequently ignore or forget responsibilities.

KEYS TO SUCCESS

- Role clarity is very important for every member of the team to make a significant contribution. As a project manager, you must mandate the use of RACI charts in your projects.
- As a project manager, you may already be using RACI charts.
- In most projects, you may prepare just one RACI chart: either at the project level or at the team level.
- At the project level, you may assign team responsibilities towards various work packages of the WBS. At the team level, your project leads may assign tasks or activities to individual team members.
- The "one RACI approach" is flawed: The project level RACI leaves the door open for ambiguity in individual roles. The team level RACI risks ambiguity in responsibilities of teams.
- Make sure you guide your teams to prepare RACI charts at both levels. This approach increases role clarity and therefore the probability of project success.

Be Culturally Cognizant

26

Ganesh was feeling good that the weekly project status call was proceeding smoothly till there was a sudden bolt from the blue. Luke, a designer from New York, seemed to be in a foul mood. He was almost screaming. "Anshul, This is the shittiest documentation I've seen. You've delivered very late. What the heck?"

Anshul, a fresh college graduate and new recruit to the team, was shell shocked. His silence further angered Luke, who demanded, "Is there a reply coming?" Ganesh didn't answer Luke directly. He moved through the next few agenda items and finally ended the call with a terse, "Thank you."

Ganesh empathized with the new recruit.

Anshul went straight to the caféteria, still dazed. Ganesh joined him soon after and told him, "What Luke did was inexcusable. I apologize on his behalf. Why was he so upset with the document?"

Anshul replied, "Jerry was supposed to peer review my manual on Wednesday. He fell sick. Since we were already late, I sent it. True, there were quality issues. But that's no reason for Luke to humiliate me in the call!"

Ganesh soothed the young man. "True, that. There was some fault on our side too. But Luke shouldn't have been so harsh. Maybe he didn't mean to be. I've seen several New Yorkers who are brutally honest with their views. But that's no excuse for disrespect. I'll certainly talk to him."

The project manager then connected with Luke for a brief discussion and explained the impact of his harsh words. He gently told Luke that the situation didn't warrant an extreme reaction. Luke said he would immediately call Anshul to apologize.

Ganesh's project was staffed by a virtual team with stakeholders and contributors from four countries in three continents. He knew that this wasn't the first instance of cultural conflict. However, severe time constraints had not allowed him to deal with these challenges.

At the project management conference he was attending that weekend, a paper presentation titled, "Respect Culture or Face Failure: Leadership Lessons from Four Continents," was presented by Karen.

She asked, "Does your project team gel well? If not, success will certainly elude you! If you, as PM, ignore this, you invite disaster."

Karen listed many categories of cultural differences that could impact virtual teams: age, geography, language, value systems, and so on. Quoting Dr. Stephen Johnson of NASA, she said, "The root causes of project failure are often cultural, not technical."

She said that her experience as a global cultural consultant showed that such situations could be reversed. Proactive leaders could leverage positive cultural traits for the good of the project.

Karen proposed a six-step process named "ASSIST" to manage cultural differences effectively: (1) Analyze team mix, (2) Search and document traits, (3) Shortlist crucial traits, (4) Implement tailored sensitivity training, (5) Stress on ethical and professional values, and (6) Test effectiveness and adjust as required.

During the Q&A session, Ganesh narrated the recent disturbing conference call and asked Karen, "How should I tackle this situation?"

She replied that an immediate apology would defuse the damage and restore balance. However, if immediate steps were not taken, conflicts would increase in frequency and ultimately derail the project.

At tea break, Ganesh requested Karen's professional assistance in turning around the difficult situation. She readily agreed to help.

Karen began with an analysis of the team's cultural mix and various traits that needed careful handling. Using customized team activities such as quizzes and role-plays, she sensitized the team on cultural differences. Karen's interventions worked like a charm as conflicts significantly dropped.

Ganesh thanked Karen as he cleared her invoice. He was delighted with how her inputs had made a huge difference to project success.

⬣ EXPERT INSIGHTS

Visukumar Gopal PMP

Practice Leader, Syntel. Founder, Viruksha Trust.

Projects in Canada, China, India, Mexico, UK, USA. **Industries:** Banking & Financial Services, Energy, Information Technology, Manufacturing, Telecommunications.

22+ years of professional experience in project/program/portfolio, process, and people management. Instrumental in driving corporate level initiatives and build competencies in operational/delivery/service/business excellence. Versatile practitioner, multipod, strategist, energetic coach, change leader, learning enabler, and public speaker. Volunteer with PMI for over ten years.

Project success largely depends on a positive cultural environment in organizations. Many projects feature virtual teams with distributed environments and multiple locations. Team members are significantly influenced by local practices and have differing world views. Diverse, heterogeneous teams and stakeholders bring with them various values, behaviors, and beliefs. Interpersonal dynamics can cause conflict even within co-located teams.

Project managers need to accord top priority to handle these factors that magnify project complexity. The goal should be to foster excellent team chemistry so that everyone works harmoniously and productively together.

Proactive project managers should devise innovative methods to leverage diversity. Such an approach can help obtain competitive advantage and improve project success.

Rene Heredia PMP, MIM, MsOD, EdD

Chief Operating Officer – MT, Inc.

Projects in China, Germany, Italy, Japan, Mexico, Poland, Spain, USA. **Industries:** Airlines, Communications, Consulting, Food & Beverage, Manufacturing, Non-Profits.

Work experience and expertise in operations, project management, manufacturing engineering, organizational development, coaching in business and change management.

When it comes to cultural differences while managing projects, the conundrum is clear: ignore them and fail or address them and take a chance. When you decide to take a chance and address cultural differences, you can choose to treat them as a burden, something you must deal with; or as an opportunity, that is, understanding and managing differences to increase success.

The first step to understand differences is by identifying our own biases and filters on the way we process information. Once we understand ourselves, the next step is to understand others' biases and filters to bridge the gaps.

KEYS TO SUCCESS

- Managing multicultural teams is a critical success factor for global projects.
- You will often work with teams of individuals who speak various languages, come from different nationalities, cultures, value systems, and so on.
- Your team members will gel well when you pay attention to cultural differences and proactively manage conflicts that may derail your project.
- Act proactively to control negativity and promote group emotional intelligence.
- For managing cultural diversity, use the six-step ASSIST process:
  - ➢ Analyze team mix.
  - ➢ Search and document traits.
  - ➢ Shortlist crucial traits.
  - ➢ Implement tailored sensitivity training.
  - ➢ Stress on ethical and professional values.
  - ➢ Test effectiveness and adjust as required.

27 Team In, Guesstimates Out

"I love Genies," an excited Dominic told himself. His manager had just informed him of his appointment as the PM for a new project, "Author Genie." The client, Selfie, a self-publishing startup, was looking to develop an author management system.

Dominic had been asked to submit time and cost estimates for important work packages in the project. He was not familiar with publishing processes. The project brief simply stated that the system developed would guide aspiring authors through the self-publishing process at Selfie.

When Dom browsed through project requirements, he found that the author management system had to include the following features: (1) log-in, (2) author's guide to the publishing process, (3) samples of various book formats and sizes, (4) cost estimates based on author inputs, (5) payment options, (6) options to select from Selfie's range of services, (7) tracking each stage in production, and (8) updates on product delivery.

Dom realized that understanding functionality in each feature was crucial. At the project kick-off meeting, he explained project scope to his team along with many areas of uncertainty. He said, "Often, we make guesses during estimation. No 'guesstimates' on this project, my friends. Which means no vague calculations. We're first going to spend time understanding details of each feature. We'll then create a detailed WBS, which will be the basis for time and cost estimates."

Dom knew that online databases and estimation tools would be of little help for his project. CEO Mark had recently sent a high-priority email to PMs cautioning against guesstimates. Pointing out that these had derailed many projects, he had asked the company's PMs to involve the team, the client, and external consultants in the process of estimation.

Putting together an estimation plan, Dom requested the client to assign a subject matter expert (SME) to explain the intricacies of every process and how it would help authors. Suman, the SME assigned by Selfie, spent two weeks with the project team. Together, they developed detailed process flow charts.

Based on these charts and other client requirements, Dom's team developed a detailed WBS. They then proceeded with detailed estimation sessions.

Work packages were shortlisted using the 80-20 rule. Dom took one work package at a time and explained all the work involved in completing it. Each team member was asked to spend a few minutes working out the time estimate. They were requested to write their estimates on Post-it notes, along with their names.

Post-it notes were arranged in ascending order of estimates.

Dom asked Basha, the person with the lowest estimate, to provide his rationale. Basha explained how automating some activities had saved 30% time in a previous project.

Leena, who had the highest number, revised her estimate downwards since she had not considered the automation.

Three Day City Tour

Did I bring too much?

Did I bring too little?

Perfect!

Wisdom of the crowd helped me get it right!

However, she pointed out challenges that had caused significant delays in a past project. Reviewing these issues, Basha now revised his own estimate upwards. Other team members provided inputs on time-saving methods and potential challenges in this work package. The estimates were tweaked till most were happy with the number.

The same process was followed for every shortlisted work package.

Team members' anxieties over the reliability of estimates decreased. Team buy-in increased. The estimation session acted as a morale booster since the team felt respected for their expertise.

Dom was very happy with a job well done. He had, after all, tasted success in estimation, an area of the biggest challenge for most project managers.

EXPERT INSIGHTS

Julio Carazo MSc, MBA, PMP

Business and Project Management Consultant.

Projects in France, Morocco, Portugal, Spain. **Industries:** Airlines, Banking, Industrial, Information Technology, Insurance, Logistics, Pharmaceuticals.

Mentor in project and business management, international speaker, entrepreneur. PMI volunteer for many years. Past President, PMI Madrid Chapter.

Predictive projects admit estimations based on historical information or "experience." What to do with new or uncertain projects?

I led an entrepreneurial initiative to build an online professional advisory service. This was in 1998, the early Internet! But WBS, PERT & GANTT had become incompatible with uncertainty.

The award-winning initiative was recognized by Harvard Business Review ("The Innovator's DNA" HBR 2009). Some learnings:

The later the activity, the smaller the effort to break it down and to estimate.

Enthusiasm, shared vision, and mission boost team creativity and performance.

Helping team members to learn, grow and succeed is a strong leadership tool.

The Agile Manifesto (2001) was knocking on the door!

Mohammad Ichsan PMP, PMI-SP, MCP

Independent Project Management Consultant.

Projects in Indonesia, Malaysia, Singapore. **Industries:** Information Technology, Telecommunications.

Experienced project management practitioner, trainer, and scholar. PMI volunteer for many years and a PhD candidate in strategic management.

Through decades of experience as a project manager in the telecom industry, I faced many challenges in the early stages of projects. In matrix organizations, project team members come from various departments and need to imbibe the project vision.

Scope, stakeholder management, and estimation are especially tough parts of the of planning challenge. Strong leadership is crucial. Thrusting estimates on team members just won't work. Instead, involving them in the process of estimation brings many benefits: (a) Team members feel respected for their experience and expertise. (b) Team buy-in for the estimates is enhanced. Most importantly, the wisdom of the crowd gives you far better estimates!

To succeed, you need to be a transformational leader and involve your team in core planning activities including estimation!

KEYS TO SUCCESS

- Estimation is one of a project manager's most challenging areas. Team involvement can make the process less difficult.
- Review estimates when the project is awarded. Assess and rectify your assumptions, constraints and high-level risks.
- Select high-priority work packages using the 80-20 rule and facilitate your team to come up with realistic estimates.
- Leverage agile group estimation techniques such as planning poker.
- Involving team members demonstrates your respect for their experience and skills. It helps you develop far better estimates and increases team buy-in.

Learning to Grow

Elva was visiting her uncle Gordon on his 70th birthday. He consulted with banks on cyber security even after retirement. Elva had often heard him say, "learning never stops." Gordon had mastered the complex domain of cyber security by continuously learning hacks and attending meetups besides reading widely and attending conferences.

Gordon's home office had a poster with Mahatma Gandhi's quote: "Live as if you were to die tomorrow. Learn as if you were to live forever." Gordon told his niece that shedding ego and asking for help was the first step in learning. His parting shot to Elva was, "In a VUCA[1] world, staying in one place is a sure recipe for facing the same fate that befell the dinosaurs."

Elva, five years into project management, was intrigued. She had realized that the breakneck speed of changes in technologies, business, tools, and techniques of project management could be daunting for many project managers. She was thinking of ways in which she could continuously learn in order to stay on top.

She sought the counsel of senior project manager, Joanne, who asked her to start with Harold Kerzner's landmark book on project management. She also pointed Elva to the PMI website[2] which had a wealth of information. Elva keenly read about the PMI Talent Triangle® proposed by PMI CEO Mark Langley which consisted of leadership, technical project management, and business skills.

Elva then jotted down the "significant few" of learning focus following Pareto's 80-20 rule that she had just learned.

1. Leadership is the number one skill for success in managing highly complex projects. Effective leadership requires soft skills such as communication, ethical behavior, presenting powerfully, negotiating win-win agreements, and practicing empathy.

2. Technical Project Management Skills: Project managers need to continually upgrade their knowledge and skills on the latest and most effective project management techniques. The PMBOK Guide® published by PMI is an excellent resource.

   Elva's thoughts were interrupted by what happened in technology. She wondered, "What would have been COBOL and Fortran in the 1980s has progressed through PowerBuilder, Oracle, Java, C++, MongoDB, Python, Hadoop, and Hive."

3. Business and Strategic Skills: Success in project management has gone beyond just delivering full scope on time and within budget. Benefits realization is critical in developing and building long-term business relationships.

4. Books are an amazing way to learn.

5. High-quality online videos, blogs, and courses are either very moderately priced or completely free of cost.

---

[1] VUCA stands for Volatility, Uncertainty, Complexity, and Ambiguity.
[2] http://www.pmi.org

"In the technology jungle get upskilled or be killed"

Elva informed Joanne that she had decided to pursue PMI's PMP® certification.

Joanne told her not to stop with that step, quoting Albert Einstein who said, "Life is like riding a cycle. To keep balance, you must keep moving."

 EXPERT INSIGHTS

Allan Mills MPM, PMP, PMI-ACP, SPC4

Director of Delivery Services, Excers Inc.

Projects in Australia, Canada, India, USA. **Industries:** E-commerce, Education, Financial Services, Government, Healthcare, Information Technology, Manufacturing, New Product Development.

Close to three decades of experience in project, program, and portfolio management systems, scaled agile framework programs, organizational change management, and systems thinking. PMI volunteer for 29 years. President – PMI North Carolina Chapter, Regional Mentor, and six years on the PMI Educational Foundation Board of Directors.

Project management is one of the most rewarding careers because of the satisfaction of delivering projects that can literally change the world. A project manager who focuses on continuous self-development and learning can literally make the world a better place.

Allowing time for regular personal reflection is the best way to grow your career and yourself. Reflect on your priorities. What do you want to continue doing well? Then think about areas of improvement. Where can I continue to learn and grow to be a better leader? How can I get a better technical understanding of my project? Where can I find ways to increase the energy of the team and excitement for the work they are doing?

These questions lead you down a learning path that enables you to improve in the priority areas of improvement. Regular reflection trains your subconscious brain to stay focused and prioritize work when the magnitude of tasks and communications seems overwhelming.

Meera Venkat MBA, PhD

President, Raise Global.

Projects in Australia, France, Germany, India, Singapore, Thailand, UAE. **Industries:** Airlines, Automobile, Banking and Insurance, Engineering, FMCG, Government, Hospitality, Information Technology, ITES, Manufacturing, Telecommunications.

Meera is a seasoned value-creator, growth, and innovation professional with experience in new business models, expanding business into new markets, and launching new businesses. She has been an advisor for several Government of India initiatives in education and technology. Future of India and CNBC presented Meera the Business Excellence Award (2016). She also won PRI's Best Women Achiever Award (2013). She is chairman of ISTD's Bangalore chapter, and executive committee member of NIQR.

When learning stops, career growth can come to a grinding halt!

Continuous learning is not easy to embrace. In competitive workplaces, managers need to work very hard to keep their jobs, leave alone get promoted! Where is the time for learning?

In my two decades heading reputed training organizations, I found that managers who consistently improved their skills progressed much faster than those who didn't. Core competencies in the modern world include leadership, technical, and business knowledge.

Employers frequently sponsor managers for training. Success chased managers who immersed themselves in training, gaining valuable knowledge and skills. Those who went through the motions, absorbing nothing, stagnated.

The good things in life are worth the sacrifice. Continuous learning is no exception!

KEYS TO SUCCESS

- Expect and plan for rapid change and volatility in business strategies, technologies, and project management techniques.

- "Never stop learning," and "continuous learning" are not just overused clichés. Your career success depends on learning.

- Develop your ideal skill set as a project manager by following PMI's Talent Triangle.® It advises that you develop a combination of technical, leadership, strategic and business management skills.

- Constantly scan your environment for the latest trends in your industry. Invest time and effort in learning about new tools and technologies.

- Leadership skills are critical for project success.

- You can also fortify your business management expertise by reading books and accessing authentic online material.

- In the agile XP practice, "pair programming" is a technique that helps people to reskill or upskill informally.

29 | Yours Truly

Thiago and Chris, best friends in graduate school, had seen their careers take them to many different cities. They now worked in the same town and shared the same profession: project management.

They met once a month for lunch at their favorite Greek restaurant and shared their stories.

During lunch, Thiago sensed that something was bothering Chris. Even over phone in the past two weeks, Chris had sounded a bit down. Thiago asked, "What's up buddy? You've seemed out of sorts for some time now."

Chris was indeed troubled and badly wanted to talk. Thiago was the one person he could really trust. He said, "You're right, my friend. I'm having a tough time. My customer doesn't trust me. Even worse, my team members seem to hate me. I feel I'm under attack from several fronts!"

Thiago encouraged Chris to open up. "Tell me more," he said.

"In my latest customer status report, I didn't disclose a delay with a critical work package. A draughtsman suddenly fell sick, and I didn't want to panic my customer. I was sure that the delay would be made up before the next fortnightly report. I showed its status as green when it should have been yellow. The draughtsman didn't recover in time, and the drawings were further delayed. Someone from my team ratted me out, and now the customer questions every minor detail in my reports!"

Chris paused to sip his drink and continued.

"I'm terribly understaffed. I have no option but to drive my team hard to stay on schedule. If someone makes a mistake, I don't mince words. I don't mind being rude if that approach gets me results. On Wednesday last week, I overheard two of my team say that I was one of the worst bosses they ever had. My woes seem endless!"

Thiago realized that the situation was worse than he had anticipated. He spoke reassuringly to Chris: "I would feel the same way if I were in your place. Don't be too hard on yourself. We can work this out.

"You know me. I don't sermonize, but it looks like you have a serious trust issue with your client. I too faced a similar situation with a delayed deliverable. I made the same mistake of reporting inaccurate progress. It looked like a small untruth at that time. Several such small untruths soon added up to have significant consequences in broken trust.

"I soon realized that it is better to be completely honest with the customer. Don't just go to them with reasons for delays. Explain your plan to get back on track. Believe me. They'll understand and grow to trust you."

Thiago recalled a leadership workshop he had attended a year back. The trainer had spoken about the importance of project managers being completely transparent and respectful with all stakeholders. He had referred the participants to PMI's Code of Ethics and Professional Conduct,[1] which stressed four important values: responsibility, respect, fairness, and honesty.

"Yes, she's very ethical and transparent!"

"Pushing your team members too hard and being rude to them may get you short-term results. But in the long run, many of your team members may push back or quit. You will lose a lot of time in finding and training new personnel.

"Take responsibility for your behavior. Don't blame the schedule. Invest time in teambuilding. Explain the challenges of your tight schedule and request their help. This way, you will get their buy-in."

Chris thanked Thiago for talking sense. Now that he had a way out of his troubles, the Greek food on the table tasted a lot more delicious.

EXPERT INSIGHTS

Mike O'Brochta BSEE, MSPM, PMI-ACP, PMP

Projects in Hungary, Tanzania, USA. **Industries:** Adult Education, Commercial, Government, High-Tech Development.

40+ years. High complexity top secret programs and projects. Organizational maturity and performance. Keynote speaker and author. Volunteer: Chair, PMI Ethics Member Advisory Group. Member of the Board of Directors (BRMC), Boy Scouts of America.

As a project manager, where my levels of formal authority were not commensurate with my responsibility, a key to my success has been leadership. And, I have found that transparency has allowed me to build levels of trust needed for effective leadership. By providing equal access to information to authorized individuals, by employing an open decision-making process, and by sharing both the good and the bad, trust levels increased to the point where I could motivate project team members, stakeholders, and others to perform as needed for

---

[1] http://www.pmi.org/-/media/pmi/documents/public/pdf/ethics/pmi-code-of-ethics.pdf

project success, especially in environments where there were competing demands placed on their time.

Sasi Kumar I.S.P, ITCP (IP3P), PMP

Projects in Canada, USA. **Industries:** Private and Public Sector.

Sasi is an accomplished information technology and project management professional with over 35 years of progressively responsible experience. He is an ardent believer in volunteerism, having been involved with PMI, CIPS, and ISO for the past 15 years. For these organizations, he has served in various member advisory groups and technical committees. Sasi is an evolving writer who shares his views on several contemporary issues including project management.

Project managers are often confronted with certain dilemmas. Questions such as "What do I do?" "Is this right," or "What if" need to be answered on a daily basis.

Such ethical issues can negatively impact not only individuals but organizations too. Dealing correctly with ethical situations requires courage and inspired leadership. Other must-have qualities include following a strict code of conduct, setting ethical standards, and being respectful in all dealings.

Lastly, but importantly, ethical performance shouldn't be random, sporadic, or on an "as you please" basis. It needs to be every day, normal behavior to duly fulfill your obligations to the organization.

KEYS TO SUCCESS

- Ethical and professional conduct is crucial to achieving project success.
- Communicate honestly and transparently with all your stakeholders, especially your customers.
- Take responsibility for your actions and decisions.
- Treat all your stakeholders with fairness and respect.
- PMI's Code of Ethics and Professional Conduct emphasizes the key values of responsibility, respect, fairness, and honesty.
- When you live by these values, you will be able to build trust, which is a vital contributor to the productivity and success of teams.

Fun with Risks

Mike was excited and anxious at the same time. The new project he was leading involved converting an existing Android app to the iOS platform. Since WeGetMobile had never executed similar work before, this project presented risks of novelty, skill gap, and lack of past data. The long-time customer was insistent that WeGetMobile take on the project since they did not want to take the risk of engaging a new service provider.

As a project manager, Mike had experienced significant success with effective risk management in past projects. But risk identification sessions had posed major challenges. Although these sessions were valuable, the meetings to discuss them turned out to be tedious.

Mike wanted to make his risk identification sessions more interesting. He connected with Randy Black, an accomplished project management best practices consultant with whom he had worked before. The veteran shared his experience with a facilitated technique designed to maximize team productivity:

"For the first 15 minutes, we work with the team to brainstorm categories of risk.

"We then identify project-specific risks using a technique called the 6-3-5 (six individuals per team, three risks per round, five minutes maximum per round)."

Randy added that this technique was developed by Helmut Schlicksupp as documented in his German book, *Kreativ Workshop*.

He continued, "In this technique, each person has a blank paper provided to them. In the first round, they write down three project-specific risks that they feel could occur. After five minutes or less, the team members rotate their page to the person on their right.

"Another round starts. Each team member reads the risks written by others and then writes three additional risks on the page in front of them. Two rules – don't repeat a risk you wrote, and don't repeat a risk that you read.

"The rounds continue until each person has their original page in front of them. In approximately 30 minutes, 108 risks (6 rounds × 3 risks × 6 pages) have been identified. Everyone then places the 18 risks on their page onto 18 Post-it notes. These are placed randomly onto a blank wall in the facilitation room."

Randy explained that over the next 15 minutes, the team would align the risks using a "silent Hoshin" method (grouping risks into "like" categories). Hoshin had been defined as the application of the plan-do-study-act model to the management process and was considered part of the inclusion steps of the Deming cycle.

During the grouping, the participants would approach the wall of Post-it notes. Without speaking (therefore the silent), they would group the risks into categories, without naming the groups.

Mike was very impressed. He was sure this method would be handy for small groups. Looking for ways to identify risks in larger groups, he called Kumar, another risk management expert he had worked with in the past.

Kumar was more than happy to help. Mike explained Randy's technique. Kumar felt it was simple, elegant, and effective. Mike wanted to understand how he could engage larger teams in the risk identification process.

"Tell your team members that together, they will entertainingly identify risks. Make it fun. Tell them that colorful sticky notes, candies, contests, and leader-boards will be featured at the meeting. Announce a risk category. Ask colleagues to write down as many relevant risks as possible in 10 minutes. They write risks on separate sticky notes, adding their names to each note. Tell them that each risk will need to be at least eight words long to make it easy to track.

"Team members who identified the most risks in each category will win prizes. Risks in sticky notes are collated, combined, and added to the project risk register. Do this well, and your colleagues will no longer feel risk identification is a dreary exercise."

Kumar concluded, "More importantly, they feel respected since their inputs and ideas are valued. They are more confident since they now believe that key project risks are being identified, with possible responses in place!"

Mike had enough ideas to implement now. He was sure that his future risk identification sessions risked no boredom!

EXPERT INSIGHTS

Randall T. Black P. Eng., PMP

President, Edutainer53 Consulting Ltd; Director, PMI Board of Directors (2017).

Projects in Canada, USA. **Industries:** Anagogical Training, E-Learning Development, Group Life and Disability Insurance, Regulated Electrical Energy, Telecommunications.

40+ years in PM Training and curriculum development and delivery, strategic planning, process improvement/re-engineering, project management.

I have found that project teams find the identification of risks, the qualifying, and then quantifying of them to be an arduous task. By making the exercise "entertaining" and by respecting their limited time, I have observed that they will enthusiastically participate. The use of the 6-3-5 and silent Hoshin techniques both intrigues (who isn't intrigued by something developed by Helmut Schlicksupp?) and respects their time. It creates a win-win-win (you get your task accomplished, you improve risk management, and you respect their time – where is the downside?) out of something that has, previously, proved to be arduous.

S. Chandramouli PMP

Associate Director, Cognizant Technology Solutions.

Projects in Egypt, Japan, India, Middle East, UK, USA. **Industries:** Banking, Finance, Insurance, Healthcare, Retail.

An alumnus of IIM Kozhikode, and Certified Global Business Leader from U21 Global University. 20+ years of experience, including 15 years in project/program management. Author of *PMP Certification Excel with Ease, PMI Agile Certified Practitioner Excel with Ease, Software Project Management,* and *Software Engineering.* Past President, PMI Madrid Chapter.

Risk identification and planning are an essential part of project management. Risk management activities start as soon as the project charter is finalized, and in some cases, even earlier. Making risk identification and risk planning sessions fun is critical in stressful project environments. Imagine the entire project team waking up each morning looking forward to the fun they will have at work that day! Interesting, right? By making risk management fun, we are mitigating risk management in a positive way. The impact of a positive and fun work environment on employee engagement is the need of the hour. Driving engagement requires adjusting work environments to make it fun, and it also influences organizational commitment. Let's make risk management fun.

KEYS TO SUCCESS

- Effective and practical risk management is a critical project success factor.
- One of the first steps you will take is risk identification.
- You can make risk identification sessions far more effective by making them exciting and fun.
- For small groups, use the technique suggested by Randy Black to gather and collate as many as 108 risks in under an hour. The technique is described in this chapter's storyline.
- For larger groups, use colorful sticky notes for team members to write risks on. Make the exercise competitive by handing out small prizes.
- Announce the names of contest winners by email to everyone in the team. This step will boost confidence by demonstrating the extensive nature of risk management in the project.
- In agile projects, the product backlog is prioritized based on what is identified as "high value" and "high risk" by the product owner. The "adjusted backlog" is used while planning. "Risk burndown charts" are used to track risks.

31 Trusty Bases

"**I**s this a joke?" Victor asked. Mano was taken aback by the sharp tone of her usually mild-mannered boss.

Victor continued, "Your estimates are too high. You're adding large buffers to make your performance look great at year end!"

Mano tried to justify the numbers: "Because there are very risky activities, I've added reasonable buffer time, Victor. Moving forward with aggressive estimates can hurt us badly later."

Victor was not in a position to listen: "There's no way Suzanne will approve this timeline. Don't you remember last week's call where she made it clear we had to complete this project in eight months? Your estimates will push that to well over eleven months. I want you to reduce all these estimates by around 40%. Please get back to me with the revised numbers immediately."

"I'll not let Victor indiscriminately cut my estimates again," Mano told herself, as she remembered a forgettable past conversation.

She had grown wiser with experience. Over the year, she had thoroughly researched solutions to the widely prevalent challenge of trust deficits between sponsors and project managers. She had spoken to Klaus, one of her former workshop trainers, asking him about possible solutions.

Mano came to understand that some project managers usually added significant buffers to their estimates since they believed that their bosses would make sharp reductions. Knowing this practice, senior staff made it a norm to advise severe cuts as the prevailing assumption was that the project manager had included large amounts of padding.

This played at the back of Mano's mind and led her to think, "How do I break this cycle of distrust?" She reviewed the advice that Klaus had sent in an email:

1. Find the "significant few" work packages that constitute a large part of the project schedule or budget.
2. Access past project data on actual time taken and amounts spent. If past data is not available, you can access data from commercial databases.
3. Where applicable, apply proven mathematical techniques such as PERT to fine-tune estimates.
4. Involve team members in the estimating process. Use relevant techniques such as planning poker.
5. Add reasonable contingency reserves to allow for risk.
6. Attach detailed bases for each estimate when submitting them for approval.

Mano did her homework thoroughly and implemented these steps in her new project. In the case of repetitive work packages, she accessed and analyzed data from past projects. Where new tasks were involved, she realized that the planning poker technique would not work with her large team of subject matter experts (SMEs). Instead, she held brainstorming sessions with her team to arrive at good estimates.

Mano had prepared her estimates as a detailed spreadsheet. She added several sheets to the file, one for each major work package. She included a summary sheet with links to the bottom-line numbers of every detail sheet. She added a comments column indicating where each estimate came from.

When Victor wanted a 40% reduction, she calmly told him that would be too much and patiently explained her estimates. She asked Victor to have a look at the Excel sheets.

The Basis Bridge can fix the Trust Deficit!

Victor was impressed. He could now verify the detailed calculations behind each estimate. The calculations showed him that Mano's numbers were not "guesstimates" produced out of thin air. The buffers added seemed reasonable as the project team had been transparent about the percentages added.

Victor asked for a day to study the estimates and then corrected a few erroneous assumptions. They were minor changes, but they significantly improved the numbers. The next day Victor approved the finalized estimate.

Over the next few projects, Victor came to trust Mano's estimates, breaking the vicious cycle of distrust and giving way to a virtuous cycle of trust.

EXPERT INSIGHTS

Patricia A Robertson PMP, Six Sigma Black Belt

Projects in Canada, China, India, Japan, Philippines, USA. **Industries:** Automotive, Banking and Card Services, Consumer and Retail, Logistics, Telecommunications.

25+ years leading global projects in contract negotiation, strategy implementation, PMOs, delivery, governance and change management. Graduate of PMI's Leadership Institute Master Class 2012. Volunteered as VP (Finance) and Chapter President with the PMI South Western Ontario Chapter. Executive Board member with the London Chamber of Commerce.

It's been my experience that many project managers are worried about being completely accurate with the scheduling and the "art" of adding buffer has gone completely off the rails adding both time and cost to the project.

Some success has been achieved in minimizing schedule risk with only applying buffer to the overall project timeline versus at the individual task level. This way, you can see a truer picture of how well you estimated, particularly at the task level as the buffer is not added there. Better overall for avoiding the student syndrome, historical purposes, and lessons learned activities.

Ammarah Shahzad MSc, PMP, PMI-RMP

Senior Project Engineer, National Engineering Services Pakistan (NESPAK)

Projects in Pakistan, Qatar, UAE, UK. **Industries:** Construction, Government.

12+ years of proven track record in all facets of project management, project coordination, construction management, contracts management and business acquisitions. Volunteered with the PMI Lahore Chapter as VP – Volunteer Development.

Many public sector projects in Pakistan are politically driven and are expected to be completed before the end of the ruling government's tenure. This scenario creates a situation of mistrust between the sponsor and the project implementer.

I have found that it really helps to have the project divided into a number of sub-projects, each of them correlated with the relevant fiscal year. This can help us effectively manage time buffers.

When time buffers are cut to low levels, project managers should focus on top-down project management. They should recruit highly skilled human resources and keep them motivated through effective team building. In arriving at the project budget, make sure you build in cost buffers based on risk contingency calculations. This way, you can convince sponsors and avoid massive cuts in the budget.

KEYS TO SUCCESS

- Increase the accuracy of your estimates and thereby boost the probability of project success.
- A cycle of distrust is possible when your team adds high time and cost buffers to estimates, with sponsors then making significant reductions.
- Carry out a Pareto (80-20) analysis to determine the "significant few" time and cost estimates that add up to a major portion of your project's schedule and spends.
- Determine accurate estimates by analyzing past data, calculating PERT estimates, and leveraging the wisdom in your team.
- Submit detailed information and calculations with your estimates for approval.
- These bases of estimates that you provided can provide better visibility to your sponsors, and be the first step in breaking the cycle of distrust.

From War to Peace

Elva had faced many unnerving situations in her last two projects. This time, she was even more worried.

Two project leads almost came to fisticuffs on disagreement over schedules in one project. One of the leads had felt that the other team's delayed deliverables were wreaking havoc with his schedule. In the next instance, a shouting match between the team lead and a team member was on show since each had a different viewpoint on the visual effect of a mobile screen. Both situations had precipitated to a danger zone. Elva had to fight these fires apart from tackling several challenges dealing with demanding stakeholders.

In the first conflict, Elva was unsuccessful in getting both sides to negotiate a mutually acceptable solution. When no agreement was reached, she spoke to her boss and shifted one of the project leads to another project. In the second, she held a "ceasefire" meeting which took close to three hours. The warring parties had finally agreed on a middle road.

Though these were situationally sensible decisions, Elva felt uncomfortable. She realized that when a shouting match between two members happened in public, the entire team was distracted. Several hours of productivity were lost. Elva was unhappy that she had not noticed the simmering discontent early on.

When she was assigned the next project, Elva was determined to keep conflicts at bay with effective conflict resolution strategies. As she researched for information on resolving conflicts, she saw an article that opined, "Nipping problems in the bud or mitigating saves much time and trouble later."

Elva read what Bruce Tuckman wrote on five distinct stages that teams go through – forming, storming, norming, performing, and adjourning. Conflict resolution was especially important in the forming, storming, and performing stages.

She read more about Tuckman's thesis from another published paper presented at a PMI conference: "Conflicts are at the highest during forming and storming. During forming, team members are getting to know each other. Lack of familiarity causes low levels of trust. During storming, many attempt to exert their dominance, trying to demonstrate their value to the team. It is critical for the project manager to do everything possible to contain conflicts at these stages. A set of ground rules should be

Their violent argument is attracting much attention & causing so much distraction!

They're focusing on each other. If they focused on the issue, it would have already been resolved!

developed. Steps should be taken to ensure that all team members understand and follow these ground rules."

Elva laid clear ground rules for her team. She made it clear that whatever be the disagreement, there would strictly be no physical fights. Any argument had to be discussed constructively in polite tones. Elva had to be informed promptly if negotiations did not bring about a resolution. No team member would intervene in any disagreement unless they could help resolve the conflict.

The approach worked. Where team members did not follow ground rules, Elva proactively reinforced the agreed-upon ground rules.

Although minor issues did go to the negotiation table, serious conflicts were avoided. At project completion, Elva was delighted that her conflict resolution strategy worked.

 EXPERT INSIGHTS

 ## Mohammad Ashraf Khan M.Sc, B.Sc, PMP

Project & Program Management Advisor at Kabul Municipality.

Projects in Afghanistan, UK. **Industry:** Government.

7+ years of experience in capacity development, change management and implementing global project management standards. Volunteering with the Project Management Institute as President of the PMI Afghanistan Chapter.

The best way to deal with conflicts is to quickly identify and effectively manage them.

Having clear rules and regulations with regards to utilizing resources, formal project management methodology, and roles and responsibilities can greatly reduce conflicts.

Low team morale is also a contributor towards conflicts. In such a case, the project manager should better work on the underlying cause (morale), rather than directly confronting or controlling conflicts.

At times, project-related conflicts might directly result from office politics where some employees might not fully cooperate with projects managed by a competing individual. In such cases, the organization should place a better performance measurement system for its employees and give greater autonomy to individual project managers.

Chakradhar Iyyunni PhD

Faculty, L&T Institute of Project Management.

Projects in India, USA. **Industries:** Construction, Information Technology, ITeS, Medical, Nuclear Equipment, Oil & Gas, Pharmaceuticals.

Over the past six years, derived insights about people behavior in projects, and quantitative management of risks. Published nine project management papers and eight large case studies. Presented three invited seminars and three external courses on risk in addition to courses as visiting faculty at NITIE and CEPT Universities. Supported three doctoral dissertations in project management and co-guided five masters theses.

I opine that managing emotion and mood is critical for team performance. At a basic level, I constantly carried out a "Trust" check and earned trust by creating value for my young team. Managing team emotion (which is like today's weather) is easy by understanding unmet needs and the parent-child – type role interactions. We understood that Gaurav (a team-member) was very emotionally intelligent and had him sort out any conflict. Maintaining team mood (which is like the climate of any place) is very tricky.

1. *Primarily, ensure that team members find it safe to speak and act. Safety is usually at risk when there is no fun or joy at work. We always had a lot of food available in the team space and occasionally adjourned to the canteen for a group singing break.*

2. *Create an environment where people find growth, meaningful work, and are provided autonomy. Growth involves assigning challenging work, with adequate support. Project managers must strive to make team members understand that all work is meaningful. Achieving autonomy requires instruction with independence. Leave was automatically approved if given a 3-week notice (not the norm in the IT industry in 2007). Team members were asked not to stay beyond shift timings. Balance of work was considered the project lead's responsibility.*

The above understanding helped us transmute conflict to (productive) confrontation.

KEYS TO SUCCESS

- Improve the probability of project success by taking proactive steps to avoid, identify and resolve project conflicts. Adopt a multi-step approach.
- First, identify the primary cause of each conflict.
- Apply the following time-tested conflict resolution principles:
  - ➢ Openness and transparency help resolve conflicts.
  - ➢ Focus on issues over personalities.
  - ➢ Not all conflicts are bad. Some can force a search for value-adding alternatives.
- In agile projects, retrospectives are used to achieve effective conflict management. They help separate people from issues, with team members making a genuine attempt to identify challenges and areas for improvement.

33   Deadly Double Whammy

G okul's organization was seriously affected by frequent project time overruns.
"We just can't believe it," said Gokul in the project managers' meeting.

"We gave team members the freedom to estimate their tasks. However, most of them still failed to complete their deliverables on time. We added substantial buffers for every module. But our project was still delayed by several months! How could this happen?"

Enter Bjorn, an accomplished project management consultant who was hired to analyze and suggest solutions to this challenge.

Bjorn asked Gokul and his module leaders to describe how the team calculated estimates at the task, work package, module, and project levels.

Salman, a module lead, replayed a conversation with one of his team members: "Vinay, let's write these four use cases next. How many days will this task take? Give me a safe estimate, but be 100% sure that you'll complete within that time. Or else…

"My final pause made the consequences sound ominous! Faced with this threat, Vinay added a few days to his original estimate. Once I got estimates from everyone in my team, I totaled them up and added a 25% buffer."

Bjorn asked Salman why he added 25% more when he knew that each team member already had buffers for their tasks. Salman replied that he wanted to make sure that he met time commitments to Gokul.

The consultant turned to Gokul: "What would be your next step after you got estimates from your module leads?"

No guesses here. Gokul too added a buffer on estimates of the team leads. He, after all, had to meet his commitments to the sponsor!

Bjorn smiled. He said, "I'm sure you've now realized how buffers at the individual contributor level get multiplied when module leads and the PM add their own safety cushions. Add all the buffers up, and you'll realize that your project had much more than what was needed.

"Do you know why team members were frequently late on their deliverables? Or why your project was still terribly delayed?"

No one knew why. Bjorn continued, "We just dealt with the problem of hugely inflated buffers. Enter the second deadly problem, the student syndrome. We're all prone to procrastination.

"Think back to your school and university days. One of your professors gave you an assignment due in three weeks. You estimated that it would take you three days to complete. When did you start? Three days before the deadline!

"I did too!"

Bjorn explained that team members, faced with severe time constraints, often postponed working on tasks to the latest time possible. If unanticipated challenges came up, their deliverables got delayed since all buffers had already been used up. All these delays added up to delays in completion of modules and further delays in project completion.

He added that very few projects and project managers could recover from this double whammy of inflated estimates and the student syndrome!

Gokul complimented Bjorn on his clarity and asked, "But what's the solution?"

The consultant explained that an excellent solution was proposed by Eliyahu Goldratt in his book, *Critical Chain*. The solution called for eliminating large buffers at work package levels and actively looking for resource dependencies that could affect the project.

Bjorn continued. "Cut down buffers at the level of individual activities. To accomplish this, you'll need to ask individual contributors for relatively aggressive estimates. Habituated for many years with large buffers, they may be uncomfortable. Assure them that, in the rare case of unforeseen challenges, delays are sometimes acceptable.

"It takes some time for the project team to get comfortable with this new approach. Once they're used to it, work pace accelerates. Team morale improves when activities are completed at a faster pace."

I'm fine... I have enough buffer balloons!

Hey there! Your remaining balloons will soon blow out and your flight will time out!

Gokul was impressed with the solution but was still not entirely convinced. He asked, "Is it all so easy? Isn't it dangerous to eliminate safety buffers? What happens if unexpected challenges crop up? Won't our compressed schedules get inflated, taking us back to square one?"

Bjorn had dealt with these questions from several other clients. He calmly explained, "Instead of buffers at the task level, Goldratt's theory recommends buffers at critical points in the project schedule where resource constraints can cause delays. These are called 'resource buffers,' 'feeding buffers,' and 'project buffers.' They provide time cushions to protect against unanticipated delays."

He concluded on a motivational note: "Learn and apply the principles in Goldratt's book. Avoid the deadly double whammy and jump on the road to timely delivery!"

⬡ EXPERT INSIGHTS

Gary Hamilton PgMP, PMP, CSM, ITIL, SSBB

Senior Vice President (Senior Change Manager), Bank of America.

Projects in Austria, Brazil, Canada, China, Japan, Spain, UK, USA. **Industries:** Banking and Finance, Consulting, Information Technology.

Senior Manager in programs, transformation, and process improvement with 20+ years of rich experience. 10+ years as a PMI volunteer. PMI Distinguished Contribution Award Winner in 2012.

Projects by their very nature create something unique. In estimating, it is vital to engage the right team member who will perform each task. It is even more critical to ensure you implement proper risk identification processes. This risk identification process should include identifying schedule risk including examining and reducing unreasonable large buffers. This critical step will help avoid the student syndrome. One of the easiest and most effective risk identification tools is a daily stand-up meeting. These meetings can be used in conjunction with any methodology to identify schedule and other risks.

During daily stand-up meetings, the progress of predecessor tasks will provide insights on the risk of successor tasks and the estimated durations. By itself, this approach may not provide as much advanced notice as one would like. However, it is extremely effective when used in conjunction with other risk identification techniques such as peer reviews of estimates by subject matter experts.

VTCS Rao B Tech, M.E., PMP, PMI-RMP, FIE, FIOD, FRICS

Dean at L&T Institute of Project Management.

Projects in Australia, USA. **Industries:** Energy, Hydrocarbons, Industrial and Infrastructure, Power.

34+ years. Strong experience in executing large capital-intensive projects in the engineering and construction industries. Handled projects across the globe from Australia to the Americas.

In the construction industry, padding is often an issue with cost estimates, not much with time estimates. If not questioned and checked, padding could lead to inflated cost and pricing, and we may lose the bid.

Project schedule development in the EPC industry is, of course, a different issue. Time estimates are adjusted to meet challenging and often overly optimistic completion schedules of clients. When committed to such large schedules, contractors should examine what they can do differently to manage such schedules. They can leverage improved work processes or new technologies. The student syndrome seems a common phenomenon across industries, especially when resources are shared across multiple projects. Things get done at the last minute, leading to both quality as well as schedule problems.

KEYS TO SUCCESS

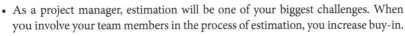

- As a project manager, estimation will be one of your biggest challenges. When you involve your team members in the process of estimation, you increase buy-in.
- However, when buffers are repeated at multiple levels, they get significantly inflated.
- When team members include large buffers, they are likely to suffer from the student syndrome of postponing tasks till the last possible moment. Tasks can therefore get delayed despite large buffers.
- Read Eliyahu Goldratt's landmark book, *Critical Chain* which details an elegant solution to the double whammy of inflated estimates and the student syndrome.
- Avoid buffers at the task levels. Instead, allow buffers at critical points in the project schedule. These are called "resource buffers," "feeding buffers," and "project buffers."

Get Lucky

Ganesh chanced upon this summary of a forthcoming online book club discussion on prjtmgmt.com, a leading online portal for project managers: *Do challenges seem to strike you continuously and from every angle? Do you suffer from compressed schedules, limited budgets, and demanding stakeholders? Are you constantly firefighting? You may be entirely justified in thinking that project managers are the most unlucky professionals in the world!*

What if we told you that you could create your own luck? Register to learn about opportunities, an often ignored area of risk management as we discuss the book, Hello PM, Get Lucky.

After grueling routines, Ganesh had gained reasonable expertise in risk management. On every project, he made it a habit of guiding his team to identify an extensive list of risks and shortlisting the most important among them by analyzing their probability and impact. Subject matter experts in his team would then formulate appropriate responses for each shortlisted risk.

He knew from experience that effective risk management helped guard against bad luck. Wondering how it could help his team get lucky, he registered for the book club webinar scheduled for the following weekend.

In preparing for the webinar, Ganesh searched on Amazon for the terms "project management," "risk," and "opportunities." On sorting customer reviews, he noticed the fascinating book, *Effective Opportunity Management for Projects: Exploiting Positive Risk* by David Hillson who called himself the "Risk Doctor."

This is OM, our Opportunity Manager! He brings us make our own Good Luck!!!!

Ganesh bought the Kindle version of Hillson's book and began to read. The Risk Doctor explained that, for risk management to assist in accomplishing project objectives and maximizing business benefits, it was critical for processes to cover both opportunities and threats.[1] He also learned how the same processes he had been using for risks so far could be used for opportunities too. And how they could potentially help every project achieve positive outcomes.

On completing the book, he decided to implement some of the techniques he had learned. At the next project risk identification meeting, he asked his team members to actively think about project opportunities.

[1] https://www.amazon.com/Effective-Opportunity-Management-Projects-Exploiting

The team's technical architect, Rocco, suggested that the project could save money on the purchase of some expensive software licenses: "We're buying 25 licenses of CADvantage, an advanced design tool. We're paying for this purchase from the project budget. It's expensive! Each license will cost $1,200. We've allocated 30K for the purchase. Our vendor has offered an attractive 40% volume discount for a single order of 40 licenses or more."

Michelle, one of the technical leads, said that she knew of a similar ongoing project that was planning to purchase 20 licenses of CADvantage. Ganesh realized that by combining the purchases, he could potentially help the company save over $21,000, in the process saving $12,000 on his project as well! Michelle volunteered to coordinate with the other project team and the vendor for combining the two orders.

At the online book discussion session a few weeks later, the moderator asked attendees for examples of opportunities they had identified on projects. Ganesh was happy to share the example of his team achieving significant cost-savings by combining purchase orders for CADVantage licences.

Ganesh and his team identified several other opportunities in subsequent meetings. The team carried out probability–impact analysis to shortlist the most important opportunities they would pursue. Every opportunity was assigned a team member who would take the idea forward.

Over the next year, the project saved a tremendous amount of time and money by pursuing significant opportunities. They had indeed created their own good luck!

 # EXPERT INSIGHTS

Ray Frohnhoefer MBA, PMP, CCP

Managing Partner/Senior Program Manager, PPC Group, LLC.

Projects in Australia, Brazil, China, Germany, Japan, Korea, Mexico, Russia, Taiwan, Turkey, UK, USA. **Industries:** Education, Financial Services, Information Technology, IT Services.

35+ years of project, program, and portfolio management; methodologist, creative inventor, and entrepreneur. His mission is to improve the practice of project management.

PMI Leadership Institute Master Class (LIMC) graduate (2010). President, PMI San Diego Chapter (2005) and global volunteer with PMI.

On my first major project, as contributor, I watched as management led us to project failure by ignoring risks. Opportunities were similarly dismissed. The project and the company failed.

Five years later, managing my first major project, I knew we had to look at risks and opportunities. Finding reusable code was an opportunity to reduce project work by 25%. Thanks to more opportunities and risks managed, we completed the project in a year with five resources. Quality was high. Other companies were spending five years with teams of ten or more for the same work.

S M Altaf Hossain FBCS CITP, MACS CP, FCMI, MIET, MIEEE SCSA, CCNA, MCSE, CPI, CDBA, CNP

Founder Managing Director & CEO, Drik ICT Limited.

Projects in Bangladesh. **Industries:** Banking, Consulting, Government, Transportation.

Founder of Dialup, the first ISP in Bangladesh. Service provider in project management training. Delivered several successful government projects for the Railway, Road Transport Authority, Army Data Center, Police, and so on. Volunteering roles include: Founder President of the PMI Bangladesh Chapter, Founder Chairman of IEEE ComSoc Bangladesh Chapter, Founder and former Vice President of the Bangladesh Software Testing Board.

I have dual passions: project management and photography. Around two and a half decades back, I dealt with negatives in both: Risks in projects and film negatives in photography.

Project managers still tend to focus too much on the negatives. Proactively looking for the positives is also extremely important. During risk identification sessions, I nudge, even push my project teams to think about as many opportunities as possible. For those with the highest combination of probability and positive impact, team members work together on concrete steps to make them happen and to achieve the goal of the project.

On many occasions, we were able to make our own good luck. We saved a lot of time and money. And of course, the project success rates indeed increased.

KEYS TO SUCCESS

- Risk and opportunity are two sides of the same coin. The outcome of the toss stems from your competency to manage risks.
- Moving from managing just risks to including opportunities can contribute significantly to your project's success.
- Effective risk management means identifying risks, shortlisting the significant few through analysis, and formulating response plans. This deals with threats.
- Managing opportunities is a great way of creating excellent performance and hence building a bank balance of good luck.
- To pursue a few opportunities, follow the same process you use with risks: identify, analyze, shortlist, and develop response plans.
- Assign an owner for every opportunity who will take the responsibility to act on them.

35 Motivating with Risk, without Risk

Thiago always enjoyed his weekly one-on-one project review meetings with the intelligent Zhang, one of the module leaders in his data warehousing project.

One of the project's best young leaders, Zhang, had aced the Project Management Professional (PMP®) certification in just three months. He had proved to be systematic, efficient, energetic, and cheerful. He had motivated his team to deliver excellent performance. His team had gained a name for high-quality deliverables.

Zhang looked different that morning. A forced smile and drooping shoulders conveyed to Thiago that something was bothering the young man.

"Is anything wrong, Zhang?" Thiago asked.

Zhang replied, "Thanks for asking. I'm finding it very challenging to get any good work done from Kristi and Ravi. They've been assigned the important role of writing test cases and scripts. They seem disinterested, and I find them making silly errors. I've tried many ways to motivate them, but as of now, nothing is working!"

Surprised, Thiago asked, "I thought you were delighted with their work a few months back. Have you tried thinking of what changed?"

After seeming to be lost in deep thought for a while, Zhang found the answer. "Ravi and Kristi were initially assigned to data modeling. They were doing an excellent job. When three members of the test team were reassigned to another project, I had no option but to assign the duo to write test scripts. Their performance started deteriorating from then on."

Thiago seemed to get it now. Kristi and Ravi, assigned to what they considered a significant and exciting task, might have now felt that their roles were devalued. Such a role change could often cause a drop in motivation levels. He shared his views with his module lead.

I see an island! Head 40 degrees North, and we'll be out of risk!

When all else fails, a young, motivated sailor saves the ship!

Zhang and Thiago discussed how they could remedy the situation. Ravi and Kristi were normally enthusiastic individuals, always willing to help. Thiago felt that engaging the duo could help overcome the problem.

Looking at where the duo would fit in, Thiago realized that tracking of shortlisted risks was an area that needed more hands. Risk ownership was a role that was being handled by module leads. They were already overburdened. He asked Zhang, "Can we ask Kristi and

Ravi to play the risk owner's role for a few risks? It would probably entail a couple of extra hours of effort for each of them per week."

Zhang nodded and thanked Thiago. He spoke to Ravi and Kristi, explaining how risk owners played a crucial role in effective risk management. Thiago would explain the risks to them, along with early warning signs that showed imminence. The duo would then track the risks and escalate when required.

Kristi and Ravi were happy to help. Thiago emailed the team, naming and congratulating the duo for taking additional responsibility as risk owners. He added in the email that they exemplified the "can do" spirit.

The email had the cascading effect of more team members volunteering extra time for other initiatives in which help was needed.

Thiago and Zhang had killed three birds with one stone. They had solved their time constraint issues, kindled the "can do" spirit in the team, and raised motivation levels of Kristi and Ravi. They went to dine at a nearby pizza restaurant to celebrate the victory of their motivation trick.

 ## EXPERT INSIGHTS

Vittal Anantatmula PhD

Professor and Program Director, School of Economics, Management & Project Management, College of Business–Western Carolina University.

Projects in Australia, Canada, France, India, Japan, Netherlands, Pakistan, Russia, Thailand, USA. **Industries:** Education, Not-for-profits.

Taught graduate level courses in classroom, online, and hybrid models at four universities. Provided project management and knowledge management-related training in USA, Japan, and India. Published about 50 journal articles and books and presented over 50 papers at international conferences and PMI chapter events. Guided about ten PhD students globally.

In general, people develop a comfort level in status quo and prefer to avoid a change as it could be risky due to uncertainties and unknowns. It is in the mindset of people to identify risk and act proactively. An individual's approach to risk is influenced by two attributes: need for success and fear of failure. The need for success prompts an individual to take chances. Fear of failure is the opposing force, which discourages you from taking risks. However, a combination of a high level of need for success and a high level of fear of failure is required to identify and manage risks well.

R Vittal Raj FCA, CISA, CISSP, CISM, CGEIT, CRISC, CIA, CFE

Founder Partner, Kumar & Raj, Chartered Accountants.

Projects in India, UAE, USA. **Industries:** Banking, Information Technology, ITES, Insurance, Manufacturing, Services.

30+ years into the journey of unraveling the mysteries of enterprise risk management, IT governance and cyber security. Directed and managed projects in the areas of Enterprise Risk Management Framework Implementations, IT Assurance, Cybercrime

Forensics & Cyber Law Consulting, SOX IT, COBIT Gap Analysis & Implementation, ISMS Maintenance Audits, Application Controls Audit, Network & Web Application Vulnerability Assessments.

What would it be like if projects were absolutely predictable and certain? They would be boring! But for project risks, PMs would be zombies! When it comes to taking ownership for project risks, everyone ducks?! The 5% who step forward to own them become leaders!

All it takes is teaming up the project stakeholders with a sportsperson-like spirit in putting their collective wisdom to think through and provide for potential uncertainties that surround the "project match," follow through with every player playing their part to collectively turn challenges into opportunities. Do these things well, and the outcome is a project that not only delivers but delights!

KEYS TO SUCCESS

- Keep your team motivated to improve productivity levels.
- Team members need interesting and challenging tasks to keep them motivated.
- Some members of your team will, however, need to be assigned to tasks that may not be very interesting. These team members are likely to feel demotivated, especially when they were playing more interesting roles earlier.
- Actively look for ways to identify individuals with low motivation. Offer such people additional responsibilities such as risk ownership.
- Recognize your team members who accept higher responsibilities and challenges.
- With this approach, you can gain the additional benefit of building a "can do" spirit among other team members. You improve team mood. Everybody can't wait to get to work! This is the real power of involving your team and allowing them to own and manage project risks.

Feed Me a Sandwich!

Mike saw Prasad reporting two hours late for the third time in the week. Prasad was one of his project's best interface designers. The recent slide in his performance had upset Mike.

"Prasad looks utterly dispirited. His attitude and work are unacceptable," he reported to his boss Mukesh, adding that the usual zeal of the designer was long gone. The designer now seemed completely bored, even depressed. Mike added, "I had to blast the guy for the awful deliverable he submitted last week. Since then, his work has deteriorated."

Mukesh thought for a while and said, "Many people may take negative feedback badly, and this can affect their performance. Was this feedback given privately?"

"No. It was at the weekly team meeting. Prasad's poor quality deliverable delayed a critical work package by three days!"

"Google the 'Sandwich Technique,'" Mukesh advised. "The way you provide feedback matters more than you think."

In researching the topic that evening, Mike found a handy article on careeraddict.com.[1] He learned how constructive criticism was a vital skill for every project manager. The article quoted Betty Lochner as saying that effective feedback had to be at least four-fifths positive. Negative criticism caused the brain to struggle to perform at the highest levels, resulting in significant performance drops.

"Oh my God, Prasad! That last screen you designed was terrible! So many elements were misaligned. The color combination was unacceptable. You've caused a three-day delay. Make sure you fix this ASAP..."

Mike now realized how those caustic words in public could have humiliated Prasad, a person who was usually punctual and efficient.

The problem wasn't that the sensitive Prasad couldn't take criticism. Rather, he had been humiliated in front of the entire team. The good work he had delivered in the past had received no praise. Mike had temporarily forgotten the golden rule: "Praise in public and criticize in private."

He was fascinated to read that the "sandwich technique" involved starting and ending feedback with positives. Included in-between would be the areas needing improvement. With this approach, the person getting the feedback was not put on the defensive right from the start. The negative feedback was cushioned somewhat by the positive ending.

Mike went back to Prasad, apologized to him, and praised him for his excellent past performance. The gesture touched Prasad. With the negativity lifted off his shoulders, there was a marked improvement in the quality of his work.

A week later, Mike found that Siddharth, one of the technical writers, had submitted a user manual chapter with many errors in grammar and spelling. He set up a short one-on-one discussion.

---

[1] http://www.careeraddict.com/how-managers-can-use-the-sandwich-technique-in-the-workplace

"I understand the frowney and really like that you sandwiched it between smileys!"

"Siddharth, I respect your hard work and creativity. You are one of the best writers in our team, and other team members value that immensely. Your writing has been excellent so far.

"But I noticed many mistakes in the latest chapter you submitted. Is there something wrong? Let me know if there's any way I can help you. By being a little more careful, I'm sure your writing will be impeccable as usual the next time."

Siddharth said, "Those errors happened since I worked on the manual while suffering from a severe bout of flu. I'll make sure this doesn't happen again."

Mike mentally thanked his boss for the valuable advice on the sandwich technique.

 EXPERT INSIGHTS

Saravanan Velrajan B.E (CS), MBA, PGDIM

Delivery Head, Verizon Data Services.

Projects in Austria, Canada, India, UK, USA. **Industries:** Services and Telecommunications.

Over 20 years of product development experience in wireless, content delivery, and software defined networks (SDN) technologies. Provided technology leadership to teams in the areas of Cellular Wireless, WLAN, Broadband Remote Access, Content networking, and Network Management. Distinguished Toastmaster (DTM). Won the Best Division Governor award with the Toastmasters organization for the year 2012.

I recommend 4Ps to further improve the effectiveness of the Sandwich Feedback Technique:

Positive: *Communicate the feedback constructively, with the sincere intent to help the recipient.*

Prioritized: *Pick the top one or two points that will have maximum impact on the individual. Don't go with a long laundry list.*

Pointed: Make your input very specific. Your feedback should not only highlight mistakes or shortcomings, but also emphasize alternative ways of doing things, or precise corrective actions.

Personalized: Every individual is unique. Customize and package your feedback keeping in mind the cultural background and maturity levels of the recipient.

Cecilia Boggi, MBA, PMP

Executive Director of active PMO, Consulting, and Training in Project Management and Leadership.

Projects in Argentina, Bolivia, Brazil, Chile, Colombia, Ecuador, El Salvador, Mexico, Nicaragua, Panamá, Paraguay, Perú, Puerto Rico, Spain, Uruguay, USA. **Industries:** Consulting, Education, Energy, Finance, Government, Information Technology.

25+ years in leading IT projects, implementing and managing PMOs. Professor at international universities and business schools. Professional executive coach and speaker in the Americas. Volunteer with PMI since 2003. President of the PMI Buenos Aires Chapter (2011). PMI Region Mentor for Southern Latin America (2014–17).

Project managers must foster unique team culture reflecting these values: commitment, dedication, respect, and professionalism. Feedback serves as an invaluable tool, helping promote desirable behaviors and discouraging undesirable actions. Since it is far easier to praise rather than criticize, PMs avoid providing negative feedback. The results? The team may perceive the project manager as being weak. Worse, the damaging behavior or poor performance of team members may continue.

Constructive feedback is a must, but not easy to implement. Starting a chat with the negative may force the recipient to go on the defensive. Ending the conversation that way may cause lingering resentment. Begin with genuine praise or positive facets. Next, provide constructive criticism. End the conversation with encouraging words. Believe me. It works.

KEYS TO SUCCESS

- Keep your team motivated to achieve higher levels of productivity.
- Over the lifetime of your project, team members are likely to commit mistakes. Feedback is essential for project benefit and your team members' growth.
- Negative feedback should be discussed in private. Praising publicly is a great way to boost morale.
- Use the following three-step feedback process:
  - ➢ Genuinely discuss the positives first, and then the negatives. This way, the team member will not right away be put on the defensive.
  - ➢ Provide the constructive feedback, with specific examples and areas for improvement.
  - ➢ End the feedback with positives, expressing confidence that the team member will fix the issues. Sincere approaches will motivate them to carry out the changes you need.

37   The Project Countdown Clock

Dominic got up early as the first rays of the morning sun hit his bedroom window. He wasn't feeling comfortable and thoughts were racing through his mind.

His last three projects had gone down to the wire, with the team scrambling to get them done. The customer had been happy, but the team wasn't. In the month before final delivery, team members had burnt barrels of midnight oil, stretching their work hours every day.

Shiny's extended hours didn't amuse her husband and kids. Mohamed was regularly missing his family dinners. Fuying didn't have time for her regular family shopping. Murali was the only person who didn't have trouble with late hours; he stayed away from his parents, working for the first time in a big city.

At the last review meeting, the CEO said, "80% of project work seems to get done in the last 20% of the time!" The comment rang true to many of the project managers but didn't help matters. Dom's track record was impressive, with all his projects delivered on time. However, he was frustrated that almost all his projects went into feverish activity only close to delivery.

That morning, as he was sipping coffee on his balcony, he wondered whether there were any solutions to his problem. He then scanned his smartphone for the daily news feed.

As if by epiphany, he came across an article on India's Metro Man Dr. E Sreedharan. The first phase of the Delhi Metro project was completed one year ahead of schedule in 2002, the report[1] said, saving not just time but also an impressive amount of public money. Delayed public projects often overshot the budget, putting a strain on state finances. The article added:

Dr. Sreedharan inculcated in DMRC [Delhi Metro Rail Corporation] employees the importance of deadlines – and meeting deadlines. "Every day with the Delhi Metro Sreedharan reminded himself and his employees of their tough deadlines. His desk had a digital clock that counted down the days before the next line had to be completed. Similar clocks were found throughout Delhi Metro's offices and construction sites."

Dr. Sreedharan called them "reverse countdown clocks." He had one on his table. Several clocks were also prominently displayed in the project team rooms. These clocks showed the number of months, days, hours, and minutes left for the project's target completion date.

As Dom explored, he realized that physical clocks were impractical, even expensive in projects with virtual teams. He found a remedy – Clock countdown applications that injected a sense of urgency in team members.

At the kick-off meeting for the Fortress+ security project, his first action point was to have the "CountingDownTo" application on all project dashboards.

---

[1] http://www.firstpost.com/india/sreedharans-backward-clock-is-forward-looking-178857.html

Dom saw its use in real time. As each milestone (module completion) was nearing, the team members were keenly checking themselves against tasks completed. They stretched before each milestone rather than pushing at the end.

"OK, WHO'S THE WISE GUY?!"

Bingo! This project too went on time, but without the usual mad rush!

The next day, Dom noticed the countdown app showing two days left. He grinned. His favorite coffee tasted far better today!

EXPERT INSIGHTS

 Mohamed Khalifa PfMP, PgMP, PMP, PMI-ACP, PMI-RMP, PMI-SP, PMI-PBA, OPM3

Director, Consultancy, LIFELONG Kuwait.

Projects in Egypt, Kuwait, Qatar, USA. **Industries:** Business Consultancy, Information Technology.

25+ years of deep expertise in effective PMOs. PMI volunteer since 2008. Serving on the Ethics Member Advisory Group (2017-19).

Dominic's story in this Chapter reminds me of my work as PMO manager where I noticed much frustration among project managers. Though they worked hard, the PMs felt that nothing was completed on time, projects were delayed, and customers were dissatisfied. To solve this problem, I decided to apply the 80-20 rule to focus on the most critical deliverables.

All of us have experienced the student syndrome at different levels; we don't study or work hard till the few days before an exam or test.

I applied agile methods to break down the project into features. I implemented the test-driven approach to finish one deliverable every two weeks. Energized by this method, everyone in the project contributed to achieving on-time delivery with high customer satisfaction!

Brajesh Kaimal PMP

Director at Experion Technologies (India) Pvt. Ltd. Consultant at Ospyn Technologies Pvt. Ltd.

Projects in India, Japan, Singapore. **Industries:** Engineering, Enterprise Systems, Information Technology, Mobile.

Entrepreneur and an accomplished project manager with 25+ years of global experience. Led several high-energy teams. Experienced trainer and speaker on project management and leadership. Founder member of the PMI Trivandrum Kerala Chapter. Global volunteer with PMI, having served in the Board Nomination committee and the Technology Advisory Group.

Timely project completion is rare. A laser focus on meeting milestones and project completion dates is priceless. While concentrating on day-to-day task completion, teams lose track of important delayed tasks. Worse, teams lose sight of the overall project completion date.

Another major issue is a lack of understanding and incorrect reporting of remaining effort. Many project managers ask team members for "percentage complete" data. If 40% of planned effort has elapsed, team members may report that they are 40% complete. Ask them for estimates of remaining effort. They will now realize that well over 60% work remains, indicating that the task is highly likely to be delayed.

Reverse countdown clocks display the number of days and hours left to a milestone or project completion date. Besides increasing awareness of the big picture, they also help find the plans that may need revision.

KEYS TO SUCCESS

- Explicit visuals enhance the sense of urgency that in turn help to motivate and reach the desired milestones on time.
- On many projects, the student syndrome forces teams to sense urgency only at later stages.
- When your team members leave task completion to the last minute, the risk of delay significantly increases.
- You can inject a sense of urgency in team members by effectively leveraging countdown clocks. Set the clocks to the time remaining for every key milestone.
- If you find that physical countdown clocks are expensive, inexpensive desktop applications can give you the same benefits.

Socially Motivating

Elva had been managing projects for ten years now. She wasn't particularly bad at socializing. However, being an introvert and severely pressurized at work, she didn't pay attention to team members outside work.

In time, much to her embarrassment, she became the "master of mix-ups." She would ask Ravi about his mom's health when it was Claire's mom who had been hospitalized. She would ask John how the Clippers were doing, forgetting the fact that he was a Lakers fan.

After many mix-ups, she was looking to reverse the situation. As she browsed through her email one evening, she saw an email from the Project Management Institute's local chapter. The email contained details of an interestingly titled knowledge-sharing session, "Socially Yours," on the usage of social media in motivating project teams. "Exactly what I'm looking for," she told herself.

A few weeks later, Kim, an accomplished speaker, started the session with a series of questions: "Are you on Facebook? What about LinkedIn, Twitter, Instagram or Pinterest?"

Almost all participants nodded.

Kim continued, "It's clear that almost all of you are connected with your team members on one social media platform or the other. But how many of you have taken the effort to scan their profiles to learn something new about them?"

Her next slide had a quote from Dale Carnegie's *How to Win Friends and Influence People*: "You can make more friends in two months by becoming interested in other people than you can in two years by trying to get other people interested in you."

She further said, "Accord top priority to team rapport. When people gel well, team spirit and communication automatically increase, boosting the chance of project success."

Kim provided the audience these tips on how they could build rapport with team members.

1. We connect better with people who have common interests.
2. Invest time in understanding the interests, expertise, and achievements of your team members. Find new ways to connect with them.
3. Organize informal sessions which give team members the opportunity to discuss common interests or showcase individual talents.
4. Personalize individual awards by tailoring prizes to the interests of each team member.

Armed with new strategies she had learned from the session, Elva logged into her Facebook account. Having not logged in for several weeks, she was surprised to see several unapproved friend requests from her team members.

She quickly accepted the requests and sent new requests to a few other team members who were on Facebook. She took time to get to know their likes and interests regarding books, movies, music, and sports.

Elva realized how she had been a tad insensitive about feelings of team members.

Much to the surprise of the team, she started liking and commenting on posts. The very next week, Elva began a 30-minute meeting during lunch time every Friday. At these meetings, she gave team members the opportunity to talk about their interests and achievements outside of work. These meetings soon became very popular.

When checking her Facebook feed on a Saturday, Elva noticed her designer Maya's post requesting prayers for her father's scheduled heart surgery. Maya had also asked for blood donors. Elva asked the designer whether the required blood had been arranged. When Maya replied in the negative, Elva immediately sent an email to the team, requesting voluntary blood donations for their colleague's father.

When several team members responded positively either on their own or by bringing their friends for donation, Maya was overwhelmed. In the next few months, the team members began to respond positively to Elva's helpful gestures.

Very late on a Friday evening, Elva found Maya working on a critical deliverable. She said, "Go home, Maya. This can wait till Monday." She was pleasantly surprised by Maya's response: "You and our team members were with me when I needed help the most. I will stay till as long as it takes to get this job done tonight!"

⬡ EXPERT INSIGHTS

D. Venkatasubramanian Diploma in Training and Development, MCA

Founder Chairman and Managing Director, SGSA India Pvt. Ltd.

Projects in Europe, India, USA. **Industries:** Aeronautics, Apparel, Automotive and Ancillaries, Education, Electronics, Information Technology, ITES, Healthcare, Learning and Development, Manufacturing.

Dynamic leader with 26+ years of experience delivering successful projects in training and development, franchise chains, apparel, manufacturing, and dairy. Passionate about people, ideas, and delivering quality results on time and within budgets.

The criticism may be sharp, but the greatest mistake some companies make is to designate their most valuable assets as "resources." I refer to human beings in flesh and blood, people with feelings, emotions, and concerns.

Leading people comes easily to some. That is because they know the pulse of their teams. The best leaders live with them, not apart from them. A leader should know the personal interests of his team by talking to them informally or leveraging social media connections. Leaders should frequently express appreciation. Organize activities to foster team spirit and a sense of bonding among team members. Informal lunchtime events and games are excellent techniques.

Demonstrating your concern for the welfare and growth of team members brings excellent results. A simple award for the "Team Member of the Month" instills a sense of competition.

Koushik Srinivasan B.Sc. Hons, PMP

Program Manager, DXC Technology.

Projects in Australia, Hong Kong, India, Philippines, Singapore, USA. **Industries:** Banking, Finance, Information Technology, Insurance, ITES.

18+ years of experience in program management. Expertise in global delivery models, cross-cultural team management, vendor and operational management. Wears many hats: project manager, engineering leader, project management evangelist, trainer, event manager, master of ceremonies, and volunteer with the local PM community. Loves meeting new people and making professional acquaintances.

Reach out to talk to me about project management, or even football.

As most of us work with multicultural teams across time zones, effective communication becomes critical to project success. The simple one-on-one phone call is the most underutilized channel today.

"Hello, Ola, Bonjour, Vanakkam, Kon'nichiwa," These are simple words by themselves but have a great impact on establishing relationships within project teams and breaking down boundaries. This phone call achieves more productivity than multiple emails and text messages.

My secret in making calls more effective is the personal connection. I spend 5% of the time getting to know the other person, speaking of shared interests, sports, culture, or even the weather before putting the phone down! Prior interactions or social media channels are an excellent way of knowing others better. This approach goes a long way in making your communication more effective and fruitful.

KEYS TO SUCCESS

- As a project manager, invest time in understanding the passion, interests, talents, and achievements of your team members.
- Identify specific areas of mutual interest with every individual.
- Informal meetings with team members will give you an opportunity to discuss common interests and their talents.
- Personalize performance awards to individual team members. It can suit their interests like tickets to a game of baseball or cricket, concert tickets, or a book in the person's area of interest.
- A motivated team that pulls together at times of genuine need delivers success better.

39 KISS!

"**W**hy can't you keep your emails short and simple?" an exasperated John asked Gokul, who was managing a prestigious automation project for EuAm Bank. John had emailed Gokul the simple query, "Can you update me on the project schedule?" Gokul's long-winded reply read:

> *"We had an initial discussion on the schedule for 26 months on July 6, 2015. But Stuart from EuAm Bank came back after internal discussions that they would want us to have a relook and asked if 23 months is possible. This was on July 8, 2015. Then I sent a revised schedule asking for at least 24 months to you on July 12, 2015. Then Stuart and I got on Skype for a discussion on July 15, 2015. We froze the schedule at 24 months on July 17, 2015, after a few back-and-forth emails. The project is deliverable on July 12, 2017, with a grace period of two months on September 12, 2017. We are now in August, and we are sprucing up to deliver it by August 31, 2017."*

John had just been interested in knowing when the project was likely to be completed. He had wanted to slot another new project for Gokul and his team. Gokul's reply irritated him no end.

He called Gokul and patiently explained a critical rule of good communication: "The 5±2 Rule of Crisp Communications states that you should restrict your message to five points in one email. This will help you grab the attention of the recipients to the fullest. If really pushed, you can add two more points and when not necessary you can reduce it to three points."

John also added that in the world of short attention spans, no one cared to read long emails. He warned Gokul, "If you are going to write long emails, there's a good chance you will fail to communicate something important."

The manager also curtly told Gokul that he would not read any emails longer than 150 words. "Crisp communication is a great weapon in a PM's armory," John concluded.

Gokul apologized and assured John that he would shorten emails.

A few days later, it was now the turn of another PM, Maria, to make a presentation. Instead of the allotted 15 minutes, she had gone on and on for 50 minutes. Maria had 75 slides that included every detail. Not surprisingly, many attendees dozed off.

We've realized some of our project emails are many pages long.
Twitter will be the tool for all future communications.
Limit all your emails to 140 chars!

John was exasperated. He told Maria that her presentation skills needed much improvement and explained Guy Kawasaki's 10-20-30 rule – 10 slides in 20 minutes with each slide at 30 point size.

Maria promised to follow Kawasaki's rule in future presentations.

John soon put up a poster on the team bulletin board: "KISS – keep it short and simple."

EXPERT INSIGHTS

Agnieszka Maria Gasperini PMP, PMI-ACP, SDI

CEO, Leader Tango. Region Mentor with the Project Management Institute (PMI).

Projects in Australia, Bolivia, Bulgaria, Colombia, Croatia, Greece, Italy, Morocco, Poland, Portugal, Romania, Turkey, Ukraine, USA. **Industries:** Academics, Communications, Electronics, Energy Management, Finance.

Agnieszka is an energetic multilingual trainer, coach, and mentor with over 18 years' international experience in the project management profession. She is a very creative coach, trainer, and consultant who uses innovative skills to support clients in designing and delivering leadership skills courses together with coaching sessions. She has a wealth of experience in working with clients from private, public, and academic organizations. Her strong interpersonal and communication skills allow her to build excellent relations with clients across all levels.

Communication is a core competency in today's projects. "Highly effective communicators are five times more likely than minimally effective communicators to be high performers..." That is a finding of PMI's Pulse of the Profession® In-Depth Report on "The Essential Role of Communications." It is evident that poor communications just won't do.

However, too much communication can also be overkill. Too often, team members indulge in cluttered presentation slides, long speeches, lengthy emails, and reports. Stakeholders just don't have the time to read long reports.

Cut the clutter. Quickly get to the main points. Use straightforward and clear language. Do these, and you will be the effective communicator who confidently delivers project success.

Arun Kiran Ponnekanti PMP

Senior Project Manager, Infosys Ltd.

Projects in India, South Africa, UK, USA. **Industries:** Agriculture, Automotive, Distilleries, Entertainment, Manufacturing, Oil & Gas.

Arun is a project management professional with 20+ years' experience in the IT industry. As a senior project manager, he delivered successful projects and programs in four continents.

Arun served as a volunteer leader with PMI for 12+ years, with his last role being Marketing Director and Secretary General of the PMI Pearl City Chapter.

Numerous global research studies attribute unclear or improper communication to project failure. Since communication is a two-way street, it is imperative for project managers to be excellent listeners. I have had much success using the "Three C" rule of good communication:

CLEAR: *Ensure your recipients understand the most important points of your message.*

COMPLETE: *Communicate all relevant details.*

CONCISE: *Use just the right amount of detail since too much information can cause lost attention and therefore focus.*

This way, you can maximize the effectiveness of a fourth C, Communication!

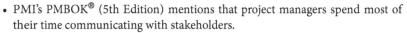 **KEYS TO SUCCESS**

- PMI's PMBOK® (5th Edition) mentions that project managers spend most of their time communicating with stakeholders.
- Effective communication is critical to project success.
- Many team members lack the ability to communicate crisply. Examples are long emails, presentations packed with congested slides, and people speaking in long monologues. Faced with severe time constraints, recipients are unlikely to absorb key points of such long pieces of communication.
- As project managers, you must coach your team members to communicate crisply and clearly.
- To maximize communication effectiveness, you can follow the 5 ± 2 rule: Aim for five points in an email or presentation slide. Limiting to three points is better. If you are pushed, you can list seven key points, but never exceed this limit.

Last Mile Connectivity

Dheeraj was excited to learn that he would soon lead a prestigious new $11.5 million project to build a premium gated community. He loved challenges.

He usually went about his work in a methodical way and put in extra effort for tricky areas like risk management. On the current project, he had spent considerable time planning for risk. His team had identified a total of 126 key risks and figured out very detailed responses.

"Dheeraj, can you drop by my office?" His boss's tone wasn't pleasant. On seeing Dheeraj, Mathew angrily asked: "How could something like this happen? Do you understand how serious this is? I thought you had all this planned out!" To his utter shock, Mathew told him that a construction worker had been seriously injured after falling through the safety netting.

Mathew asked, "How can this happen when you claim precautions for all risks are in place?" A perplexed Dheeraj could only say that he would find out the cause of the problem and explain.

The war room was soon buzzing with Dheeraj, Felix, the site supervisor, and team in a huddle. Revisiting risks, they found that there were no gaping holes. Felix gave Dheeraj the vendor list. When SafeNettings, the usual supplier, was mentioned as the vendor for safety nets, Dheeraj understood.

SafeNettings had a poor track record of below-par nets. What surprised Dheeraj was why SafeNettings was not changed despite a specific request to change the vendor though it would mean a higher price. It was a matter of lives!

He soon found that the new Procurement Manager, unaware of SafeNettings's reputation, had awarded the contract based on price.

That alerted Dheeraj to a problem of far greater magnitude. His team had done a great job identifying risks, analyzing them, and shortlisting and formulating response plans. Though the response plan was followed, the contract went to SafeNetting. Dheeraj needed to know why.

He reached out to his ever-reliable mentor Kaito Tanaka and explained his problem.

Kaito-san listened patiently and said, "You would have heard of the proverbial slip between the cup and the lip. The fault here is not in lack of planning. You missed last mile connectivity."

"But how?" asked Dheeraj.

Mr. Kaito explained, "Your team missed the link between the risk response plans and tasks on the project schedule. This miss negated the effectiveness of your excellent risk planning."

"Connecting the risks with work packages?" asked Dheeraj.

"Dheeraj, You need to understand that one formulated risk response action may apply to several similar work packages. Also, one work package could be susceptible to many risks. If your team doesn't make the connection, incidents similar to your latest accident will recur.

"Take proactive steps to make the last mile connection. Make sure your team insists on relevant risk response actions to be referred to in your project scheduling."

Thanking Kaito-san profusely, Dheeraj resolved to put his mentor's advice into action.

The next day, Dheeraj asked his team to link action items in their risk response plans with tasks on the project schedule. Work package owners were designated as risk owners. Fortnightly meetings were set up to update risk owners with changes in the risk register.

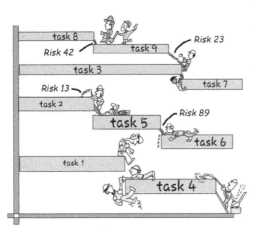

Dheeraj explained to Mathew how despite identifying the safety net risk, it did not reflect in the identification of the vendor as the risk plan was not linked to tasks on the project schedule. He also apprised Mathew of remedial action taken to prevent future problems.

The last-mile linkage gave an important lesson to Dheeraj to connect the missing links. He and his team had learned it the hard way.

Risky chains that free you from failure!

⬢ EXPERT INSIGHTS

Tejas V Sura B.E., M.S., MBA, PfMP, PMP

Managing Director, Cubic Turnkey Pvt. Ltd.

Projects in India, USA. **Industries:** Construction, Design, Procurement.

22+ years of experience in implementing PMO frameworks for program and project management. PMI volunteer since 1998. Member of PMI's ISO Member Advisory Group from 2017.

Schedule overruns are considered to be an inherent characteristic of complex projects. Most project managers are confident that project timelines can be monitored and controlled utilizing techniques such as the critical path method. My experience on construction projects has established a strong need to additionally monitor the risks and respond promptly to meet project milestones. On a complex congested work site, the risk of inability to provide road access to a crane for the erection of trusses was triggered well in advance and resulted in redesigning of trusses to enable unconventional construction methods and maintain the schedule.

Malgorzata Kusyk PMP, PRINCE2P

Mentor, Business Trainer, MBA Lecturer and Speaker Worldwide.

Projects in Austria, Bulgaria, Canada, China, Denmark. Finland, France, Germany, India, Ireland, Italy, Japan, Netherlands, Norway, Spain, Thailand, Turkey, UK, USA. **Industries:** Banking, BPO, Financial Services, Information Technology, Telecommunications.

16+ years in managing projects and leading multicultural high-performance teams. 10+ years in implementing project management frameworks, optimizing processes, and managing PMOs, combining agile with traditional approaches. Creator of several innovative business solutions and training programs. Blogger and PMI volunteer since 2008.

Linking risks with tasks on the schedule is indeed a critical activity for project managers. To ensure coverage, a kind of risk breakdown structure (RBS) should be used. It can be a WBS or "a clock" as employed in collaborative games by agile teams recommended by Mike Griffiths.

Collaborative games are powerful tools to engage the team and other stakeholders leading to a complete list of possible risks and more creative ways of mitigating them. Develop a game that challenges teams to find as many links as possible with risks on the risk register and tasks on the schedule. Make it competitive.

Both positive and negative risks are important. They need to be linked to tasks and managed proactively. Where relevant, tasks to handle risks and opportunities can be added to the project schedule.

KEYS TO SUCCESS

- As a project manager, you must understand that effective risk management can be critical to your project's success.
- Realize that a single response plan might affect several tasks on the schedule and that a single task might be affected by multiple risks. Update the links periodically to maximize the effectiveness of your risk management system.
- Identify an extensive set of risks and shortlist significant risks based on probability–impact analysis. Do not completely ignore the non-priority risks.
- Formulate effective response plans for the shortlisted risks and review often to check for non priority risks becoming important during a subsequent project phase.
- Stopping at this point of planning will negate much of the hard work put into risk management.
- Take proactive steps to make the last mile connection. Link the action items in risk response plans with tasks on the project schedule.

41   Fun and Games at Work

Ganesh was frustrated with how his project was progressing. Tight schedules gave his team no breathing space. The usual spark was missing in even the most cheerful members of the team.

The team's tense mood was causing unnecessary conflicts, taking a toll on productivity. Ganesh knew that he could not let this situation continue. He had to do something.

He spoke to his wife Preethi, an HR professional at another firm. She asked him to read the book she had recently bought: *Fun Games for Team Building & Morale Boost*. Ganesh read the book with interest.

On Tuesday, he called for a meeting with his module leads, Irfan and Jennifer. He told them, "Guys, why the heck are people stressed and tense? They unnecessarily pick up fights. We certainly need to lighten the mood." Showing them the book he had read, he said, "Let's go gaming."

Irfan and Jennifer looked at each other. Ganesh smiled and said, "This book says the fun element in games boosts team engagement and therefore productivity. I thought, 'why not give it a try?'"

Handing over the copy, he said, "Take turns reading this book. Search the web if required. Find game ideas that will work with our team." The duo gave a thumbs-up. They were game for the challenge!

Jennifer found the game "Know 'em More" interesting. She described it to Ganesh. Apart from helping team members know more about each other, it could help in higher team spirit and bonding.

She said, "I plan to email all team members asking them to reply with three personal facts they're comfortable sharing with their colleagues. These facts are not publicly known. Once they do, the game begins."

She added, "We'll group colleagues into teams that will compete for prizes. We are thirty. So six teams of five people each. Thirty questions. Teams are asked to name the team member about whom a fact is revealed as a question. We will award points for correct answers. The team that gathers most points is the winner. Then we could change it to achievements, interests, and passion of each person and continue the game."

Irfan suggested the "Tower Game" developed by volunteers of the Project Management Institute Educational Foundation (PMIef). He said, "We played this game at a project management workshop that I attended. Here's how we play:

"We form teams of four to five colleagues each. We hand out 20 spaghetti sticks, five paper cups, and one roll of adhesive tape to each team. Teams are instructed to build freestanding towers of at least 50-centimeter height in 20 minutes or less. Towers need to be stable for at least 20 minutes. We award height incentives to teams for quick execution and efficient use of the materials provided. We award prizes to the teams that built the tallest towers after adjusting for height incentives."

Irfan explained that by playing the game, team members not only had fun. They were also able to understand key project management concepts such as scope, time, cost, quality, risk, planning, communication, and leadership.

Faking a deep voice, Ganesh said, "Let the games begin!"

How come everyone's in so early today?

Today's Wednesday: The day we all play games!!!

Soon the team was greeted with "Games Day" announcement on Wednesdays. Jennifer and Irfan conducted dry runs the following week. The team simply loved playing the two games. Team members eagerly awaited Games Day every week. New games were regularly added.

Ganesh was happy to see a perceptible rise in the team's energy levels. Conflicts reduced significantly.

At a candlelight dinner with his wife that weekend, Ganesh thanked her for the gift of the valuable book that had significantly helped to improve his team's mood!

⚙ EXPERT INSIGHTS

Pablo Lledó MSc, MBA, PMP

President, Pablolledo.com & Maxi Mall.

Projects in Argentina, Brazil, Costa Rica, Chile, Colombia, Ecuador, Guatemala, Honduras, Mexico, Nicaragua, Paraguay, Peru, Spain, Uruguay, USA. **Industries:** Consulting, Education, Finance, Real Estate.

Entrepreneur (founder of five companies), author of nine books, international speaker. Volunteering with PMI: Served as President and VP of two PMI chapters. Was on the Board of Directors of the PMI Educational Foundation (2015-17). Winner of the PMI Distinguished Contribution Award (2012).

Gamification is a very effective team building technique.

The "Tower Building Game" is a simple, fun, yet intense learning experience. It provides excellent lessons in team building, scope, time, cost, quality and risk management.

Teams are provided 20 sticks (wood/spaghetti) and five paper cups each. They are asked to build the tallest free-standing tower at lowest cost while meeting quality requirements.

During the Lessons Learned session, teams answer these fundamental questions:

What is a successful project? Was time allotted for planning? Why is the tallest structure not always the best? How can teams effectively manage project constraints? How can risk management help in project success?

More information at: www.pmief.org

Simona Bonghez PhD., PMP

Managing Director, Colors in Projects.

Projects in Central and Eastern Europe, Kuwait, Romania. **Industries:** Banking, Construction, Education, Information Technology, Manufacturing, Oil and Gas, Telecommunications.

25+ years of experience in change management, project management, and adult education.

Volunteering: President of PMI Romania Chapter (2007–11), Member of the PMI Leadership Institute Advisory Group, Chapter Member Advisory Group, and Ethics Member Advisory Group (2012–17).

Serious games (games designed for a primary purpose other than entertainment) and gamification (using game-design elements in a non-game context) are great drivers for enhancing employees' motivation and raising engagement of employees, customers, or other stakeholders. When correctly applied, game design levers such as competition and collaboration, curiosity and challenge, surprise and achievements can have amazing results.

However, those who would like to be successful in pursuing such an initiative will need to follow some basic rules:

- *The games should have a clear goal and participants need to understand a reason behind playing it (Ludus versus Paidia).*
- *The design should appeal to people's emotion: there should be a story behind the game with a definite purpose.*
- *The design should address all types of players (killers, achievers, socializers, explorers).*

Having all this in mind, fun, learning, and building great teams are guaranteed outcomes.

KEYS TO SUCCESS

- Effective handling of project pressures is necessary to avoid conflicts and to keep team spirits high.
- The use of fun games and team building activities can help lighten the mood in tense teams.
- At project start, use ice breakers to help team members know each other better.
- The short story in this chapter described two proven games, a team trivia/quiz, and PMIef's Tower Building game.
- You can devise your own games and team-building exercises that can help improve team morale.

Compliment Quickly, Continuously

Deepa was a star performer, regularly winning customer appreciation and ample praise from her bosses. Not surprisingly, she often won performance awards. Dominic chose her for the next prestigious project.

Dominic sensed serious trouble with just a week left for a module to go live. Since the documentation team was way behind schedule, he assigned Deepa to the tough task of turning around the track. Deepa was cheerful, focused, and inspirational. She quickly helped the documentation team get their act together.

Dom was a man of few words. Over the next few weeks, he focused on project completion. Deepa felt neglected as her hard work had not been acknowledged. She confided in Miriam, her colleague, who advised patience. However, Deepa's frustration grew due to the project manager's indifference. She chose to go on leave for a week. Dom, while surprised at the sudden request, reluctantly approved it.

Late one day, Dom saw Miriam waiting for a cab. Since they stayed in the same neighborhood, he offered to drop Miriam home. Soon, their conversation turned to Deepa. Miriam explained how Deepa's morale drop was due to lack of appreciation. Taken aback, Dom said he had already decided to recommend Deepa for the project's best performer award.

Miriam asked Dom, "But how would have Deepa known?" She said that a previous boss Syed had achieved great results using instant appreciation to boost team motivation levels.

Dom soon reached out to Syed for advice. As they chatted, Syed quoted educationist Margaret Cousins: "Appreciation can make a day, even change a life. Your willingness to put it into words is all that is necessary."

Even the super heroes crave appreciation!!

He went on to say, "I know that people can go without food and water for days, but suffer much when not appreciated. Instant, genuine appreciation of hard work, initiative, and creativity is a powerful motivational tool. These principles are central to the well-known Fish philosophy, made famous through research into Pikes Place, the Seattle fish market. In a previous job, I was part of the leadership group which successfully implemented this program."

Syed described the instant appreciation scheme he had designed. A "You're a Star!" badge was instantly given to anyone at any time for good efforts with no restriction on the number. Anyone could be the giver or recipient, irrespective of position.

Appreciation cards were handed out for any action beyond the usual course of work: A creative idea for improvement, help with a presentation, or organizing a milestone celebration. Sized like a visiting card, these were colorful and two-sided, with spaces to fill in names of the giver and recipient, date, and the reasons for appreciation. All cards were handed over to a project administrator at month-end.

The recipient of most cards in a month was given a company-paid dinner with family in a premium restaurant. By lucky draw, a few others received gift vouchers for buying books, clothes, or gadgets.

The gifts were fun, of course. The primary value, however, was in the instant happiness at receiving an appreciation card.

As Deepa returned from leave, she found six appreciation cards waiting for her. Miriam often received "You're a Star" badges, as did all other team members.

Dom now understood the effect of instant appreciation.

⚙ EXPERT INSIGHTS

Mary Mateja

Retired Vice President – Worldwide Information Technology, Pfizer Pharmaceuticals, New York.

Projects in Czech Republic, Denmark, Finland, Slovakia, Taiwan, UK, USA, and several other countries. **Industries:** Education, Information Technology, Pharmaceutical R&D.

Experience in governance, portfolio management, and document management.

There are two concepts I highly recommend to bring out the best in team dynamics.

Recognizing the contributions of team members is vital to the health of the team. Large and small contributions all lead up to the success of a project. Each person should feel that his or her work is recognized and appreciated along the way, not just at completion. It is so easy to drop a short note at the end of the day to those who contributed something special.

My team and I had exceptional success implementing concepts of the Fish philosophy across the entire site.

I also firmly believe that the best teams understand the larger picture of what is being accomplished.

Tie their work to the big picture. When working in pharmaceutical R&D, we had a saying to inspire us to get the job done and feel connected to the outcome. The phrase was "the patient is waiting." No matter what your job was in that organization, the goal was to discover life-saving medications for those in need. It was a great motivator and kept our eyes on the prize.

S N Padmaja B.Sc. M.A B.Ed DFA DHC CHM CCBT CISTD

Chief Training Consultant, Victory Insights. Consultant, Madras Management Association for nine years.

Projects in India. **Industries:** Automotive, Banking, Education, Finance, Education, Hospitality, Healthcare, Information Technology.

25+ years of deep expertise in transformational coaching, motivational talks, counseling through media, individual coaching, behavioral counseling, effective customized HR learning and development initiatives.

Happy people are productive people. I achieved remarkable results in my projects by implementing four pillars of the Fish philosophy to foster positive team culture:

Choose your Attitude: *Attitude determines altitude. You can boost morale and increase team productivity by rewarding team members who exhibit a great attitude.*

Be Present: *As a project manager, be a shining beacon of enthusiasm and energy. This passion will rub off on your team. Results automatically follow.*

Play: *Fun at work reduces boredom. Every workshop I facilitated included many fun activities. The result: energized participants, satisfied clients, and more assignments.*

Make their Day: *Catch team members doing the right things. Compliment and reward instantly with spot recognition. Encouragement wins trust, and trust brings great results!*

KEYS TO SUCCESS

- To keep productivity levels high, you need to keep your team members motivated.

- As a project manager, you should not outsource motivation to the human resources department.

- Implement a project level reward and appreciation process and acknowledge your team members frequently.

- It is a proven fact that, as human beings, we crave appreciation. Delayed appreciation devalues the praise. You can effectively leverage elements of the Fish philosophy.[1]

- Devise your own program of instant appreciation. Make the program fun and exciting.

- When done right, motivation and appreciation can help you achieve higher levels of team morale.

---

[1] http://www.fishphilosophy.com/fish-philosophy-story/

43 Quadruple Quandary!

Elva was upset with the results of her initial project assignments. Budiwati, assigned to a key technical design task, had been so slow that the entire project was set back by days. Mikolaj had made a mess of identifying potential risks based on the requirements document.

She had spent much time talking to her team members to understand their aspirations. She had also briefly considered their experience in determining the best fit. Many assignments had worked well, but a few had failed badly. "What did I miss?" Elva asked herself.

Needing advice, Elva turned to Narayan, a fellow project manager well known for his impeccable project task assignments. After listening patiently, he asked her to analyze the possible reasons for the duo's failures.

Elva thought a while and said, "Mikolaj liked the challenge of risk identification since he wanted to learn project management skills. His biggest strength is people skills. Assigning him a task that required keen attention to detail was a mistake.

"Budiwati aspires to be a technical architect. That's why I asked her to assist with a relevant design task. She's a quick learner, but this critical path activity afforded no time for learning!"

Impressed by Elva's perceptive thinking, Narayan said, "Kudos on diagnosing your problems brilliantly. Task assignment isn't easy. You can never get it right all the time. However, I've learned from experience that some important principles apply:

"Aligning tasks with personal aspirations is a good idea. But as project managers, we should consider other key factors to match tasks with the right people: aptitude, knowledge, skills and relevant experience. This concept was emphasized by Nobel prize-winning author Herbert Simon who wrote on the 'Second Law' of Organizations. He insisted that managers use only the best person for every task in an organization/project.

"It's great that a team member wants to learn. However, we just can't risk assigning an inexperienced team member to a task on the critical path. Rather, we should assign the best possible resources taking into account the skills, attitude, and experience required for every critical path activity."

As Elva listened intently, Narayan narrated a recent experience: "As a past soccer player, I coach a nearby school team. They've won all three of their matches this year, and the temptation is great to continue with the winning combination.

"However, I realized that all our opponents so far have been strong defensive units. Next week, our team plays a much stronger opponent. They have a terrific offensive line. We have no choice but to change our line-up.

"Instead of playing three forwards, we'll play one and add two defenders. Our team's captain has all-around skills. He is a great forward but also has excellent defensive skills.

Against a more aggressive opponent, I may need to leverage his skills in the center-back position from where he can guide his defenders better!"

"Ah! the perils of being a critical all-rounder!"

Elva understood. She said, "Some of my team members are versatile all-rounders who can excel at many tasks. Am I right in assuming that I should assign them to the most critical activities at any point in time?"

Narayan responded, "You're 100% right. We can discuss more, but it's time for my next meeting. I'm sure you have enough to do a great job on the next set of assignments!"

EXPERT INSIGHTS

Farhad Abdollayan M.Sc, PMP, PMI-RMP

Global Thinker and Practitioner, Cyrus Associates.

Projects in Argentina, Brazil, Cameroon, Central African Republic, Chile, Colombia, Democratic Republic of Congo, Haiti, Iran, Kenya, Mexico, Senegal, South Sudan, Trinidad and Tobago, Venezuela, Yemen. **Industries:** Agriculture, Government, Information Technology, Manufacturing, Retail, United Nations Agency.

35 years. Enterprise resource planning, mergers and acquisitions, humanitarian, post-disaster reconstruction, organizational project management (OPM) assessments. PMI chapter officer and volunteer.

Assigning the best resources to the critical path is indeed important. From experience, I advise project managers that the critical path itself is dynamic, and in many cases, changes.

Carefully monitoring the critical path is crucial to rapidly transfer resources from a previous critical path to the new one. This action often presents a new challenge: The resources assigned to the original critical path activities may no longer be suitable for the new critical activities. How can we handle this new challenge? The secret is to prepare contingency resource plans for the near-critical paths.

Imre Szalay MSc, PMP

Consultant for Project Management and Process Improvement, CRS Plus.

Projects in Hungary. **Industries:** Banking, Information Technology, System Integration, Telecommunications.

20+ years as project management speaker, trainer, consultant, and in developing and leading project related business units. 15+ years leading Project Management Offices. Founder and President of PMI Budapest Chapter. Organizer of project management communities' cooperation in Hungary.

The real question here is how we can practically implement the theory of assigning the best possible resources to critical path activities. How do we eat the elephant? My hints are based on my practice working for and at matrix organizations.

Do you want to excel and be the best? If so, you need to demonstrate excellence in areas beyond the hygiene factors of traditional resource management, namely, stakeholder relationships, practical tools, and motivation. Here are three ideas:

Analyze and list critical resources (business process owners, system domain gurus) in bottleneck areas. Involve them in your plans and help them to survive their deadlock situations. Create flexibility and build stakeholder trust by being open and honest about resource demands. Leverage the over and underestimation trends.

Think about the bigger picture. Understand changing priorities and resource dependencies among the projects of the relevant portfolio.

KEYS TO SUCCESS

- It is critical to assign the right tasks to the right team member.
- When assigning tasks, look at the team member's skill sets, knowledge, and experience relevant to the task.
- When possible, assign tasks based on individual career aspirations.
- When you assign people to activities on the critical path or near critical path, avoid assigning inexperienced or unskilled team members. On these activities, there is no time to learn. It is important to remember that critical path activities require the individuals with the most relevant experience and skills.
- When making assignments, find the most critical activities at a particular point in time and assign those to the most versatile and multi-skilled individuals in your team.

360 Degrees of Appreciation 44

The recently concluded project management conference had been an unqualified success. Star speakers, a variety of formats, and excellent ambiance had all contributed to the success. But the real X-factor was a dedicated, passionate, and amazingly energetic volunteer team that had left no stone unturned to deliver a terrific event.

Feedback from delegates was fantastic.

Conference chair Mano knew how hard her volunteer team had worked. Though every volunteer had a day job, they had burned the midnight oil over many weekends over the past nine months to plan the conference to the last detail. The volunteer team had leveraged many project management best practices such as the charter, WBS, vendor evaluation criteria, RACI charts, and risk response plans, among others.

Big success called for a big celebration. One sunny Saturday a few weeks later, all volunteers, accompanied by their families, reached a top resort on the outskirts of the city. The kids were visibly excited as they saw stalls for face painting, tattoos, bouncing castles, and many fun games. A magician was on-site to entertain everyone.

Soft music was playing. Spouses and relatives of the volunteers, happy to make new friends, chatted and enjoyed delicious appetizers.

Surprisingly, none of the volunteers were with them. Where had they disappeared?

They were sitting in a circular arrangement in an adjoining room. Mano was right in their midst. "Speech, speech," the volunteers chorused. Smiling with pride at the team that had delivered stellar success, she said, "Guys, I sincerely thank each of you for an amazing conference. Together, we proved what a truly passionate team of volunteers can achieve. We have something special planned for you today. Something that we hope you will cherish for long!

"Our friend Koushik came up with the idea of a fantastic group activity. He has printed notebooks personalized for each of us." Mano showed a sample. The cover page had a laminated group photograph of the volunteer team on stage. An inset at the bottom left corner of the cover had the volunteer's picture. "Please pick up the notebook with your photo," she said.

Everyone collected their personalized books and sat down. Mano asked Koushik to explain what the team was going to do.

"Guys, the rules are simple," Koushik said. "Each of us will hand over our books to the person on the left. We will each take a minute or two to write something nice about your friend on the cover. Be specific. You can compliment your friend on their attitude, brilliant ideas they came up with, how they contributed to project success, and so on. You will then pass it to the person on your left. We keep doing this till everyone gets back their book. Any questions?"

"What if we run out of pages?" asked Selva.

"Don't tell me you are in exam mode!" quipped Koushik. Everyone laughed.

The 33 volunteers showered praise on each of their colleagues in memorable words, and in an hour the activity was done.

Mano, having just finished reading her notebook, was beaming. "What did you get back?" she asked.

The answers came thick and fast: "Precious praise." "Words to remember." "Comments that brought happy tears!"

"Something we will all treasure!" was the final answer.

Mano said, "As project managers, you have also learned an excellent motivational technique which you can use with your team. We call it the 'Appreciation Circle' in our project. We do this every month.

"Instead of the glossy notebooks, we use plain white sheets. When we start, each team member writes their name on the bottom right corner. After a colleague has written nice words, they fold the sheet so that the next person can write something unique. We invest around 30 minutes. Just like today, the return on that investment is priceless! Try it out with your teams. It is magical for morale!"

"One sheet is not enough!"

Mano thanked Koushik, saying, "Thanks a million for your great work with this activity! We achieved exactly what we set out to do!"

As the happy group got up to join their families, Mano was puzzled to hear the question, "When is the next conference Mano?"

She asked, "Aren't you tired from this conference? Don't you need to rest to recharge?"

The response left her overjoyed: "We've become addicted to the camaraderie and team spirit of volunteering. It's like a drug. We don't want to suffer the withdrawal symptoms!"

⬡ EXPERT INSIGHTS

Jacob Zachariah MBA, PMP

Project Management Consultant.

Projects in Canada, India. **Industries:** Banking, Information Technology, Telecommunications.

25+ years in creating PMOs for IT in banking, delivery, governance, regulatory compliance management, SDLC, and implementation. Member of the volunteer Board of Directors on the PMI Mumbai Chapter.

I experienced first-hand the implication of demotivation in a project. Shoulders drooped, and disinterest crept in among team members due to an over-interfering stakeholder and the resultant delay in deliverables. Regular stand-up meetings did nothing to bolster the sagging morale. We decided to break this routine. A Friday evening dinner preceded by music and games was arranged. A motivational lecture was also organized during the break.

Participants were encouraged to discuss and analyze the project as it stood then. The meeting went a long way in releasing bottled-up feelings, having a two-way dialogue, and identifying stumbling blocks. This informal way of communication brought the ailing project back on track.

Manepalli Vinay Babu B.Com CAIIB-1

Former Senior Vice President – Customer Centre at Kotak Mahindra Bank.

Projects in India. **Industry:** Banking.

28 years. Starting as Business Development Manager, progressed through various leadership roles including Branch Manager, Region Head, Head (Customer Experience), and Head (Customer Contact Centre). Since then, moved into chasing his dreams: Carpenter designing and hand making wooden products and cycling. Accomplished several rides for fundraising from 500 to 4,500 kilometers (Kashmir to Kanyakumari).

The officer on call is the fulcrum of every Customer Contact Centre. It is a stressful job, handling up to 150 calls a day, with targets on call count, handling time and error-free delivery. Customers range from pleasant to downright nasty.

To me, 360-degree appreciation is the process of empowering team members with the necessary power to handle customer needs and issues. The first step is to elicit continuous feedback and tweak processes as required. Accord top priority to rewarding team members for excellent customer feedback. Make this the top performance measure.

Implementing this process in my organization brought remarkable results in customer satisfaction and team morale. Attrition levels dramatically dropped. Business results were off the charts. This transformation earned me a promotion to the role of Senior Vice President. Today, the concepts put in place are continuing to fuel the growth of the department.

KEYS TO SUCCESS

- Motivated, charged-up teams produce much higher levels of productivity.
- Invest time to ideate and implement team building activities on a regular basis.
- Appreciation circles are an excellent technique you can use to build team motivation. Details are available in the storyline.
- Use variations of this theme such as gift bags with team member names on them. Each team member writes notes on specific contributions other individuals made on a sticky note and drops them into the appropriate gift bags. Team members then take the gift bags with their names home. They are delighted by the praise their colleagues gave them.
- Devise your own innovative activities. Keep them simple, fun, and motivational. Run them at regular intervals to keep team morale high.

Embrace Empathy

In all his experience as a project manager, Thiago had never felt more frustrated. That morning, his boss Dylan had reprimanded him for his "poor communication skills." Accusing Thiago of not alerting him about the project's status, he had said, "If we aren't completely transparent with each other, this project is doomed. See you later."

Since Dylan rarely lost his composure, these sharp words left Thiago lost for words. The boss had completely overlooked the detailed status email Thiago had sent the previous evening. Biting back bitterness, he grabbed an espresso and went back to his office.

An email from Solomon, one of his designers, was a double whammy for him. Thiago was shocked to know that the designer felt that he was overloaded. Solomon's curt words conveyed that he couldn't take the pressure anymore. He wanted five days off. Thiago felt like a piñata at a party.

On the way home, he called his mom Jimena, considered one of the mentally strongest people in the family. She had retired as HR head at an established engineering firm.

"A week Mom! An entire week. Doesn't Solomon realize that our project is already delayed? And then there's my unreasonable boss to deal with," fumed Thiago. "How did he not see the email I sent him? It's like the world is conspiring to make my job as difficult as possible." Jimena calmly heard him out, understanding that her son must have gone through a tough time at work.

"I fully understand Tagi," said his mom softly, her tone affectionate as usual. "I've faced similar situations myself. Understand that they probably had bad days too. Put yourself in their shoes. Why would Dylan, the boss who usually speaks highly of you, or your designer Solomon, who admires your leadership, snap at you for no apparent reason?"

His mom continued, "Think back. Could there be a reason behind their sudden irritability?"

Thiago remembered that his project's customer had sent an angry email about project delays to the division VP. Maybe Dylan had been shouted at by his boss, with the frustration spilling over to Thiago.

Solomon, the usually cheerful designer, had looked entirely out of sorts in the past week. He just recalled a status update on Solomon's Facebook wall that said, "Pray for us." Thiago suspected someone in Solomon's family should be keeping very unwell, making him lose focus and perspective.

"Yes, Mom. I realize that I'd have reacted the same way if I had been in their place," he said.

"Remember, Tagi," Jimena said, "A little empathy can take us all so much further. Keep that in mind before judging anyone's actions."

"That's why I need you mom! But what if others don't reciprocate? What if they adamantly refuse to see my point of view?"

Jimena told Thiago that there was a simple trick to making others empathetic. Faced with someone who was unreasonable and refusing to budge, he could ask, "I see where you're coming from. Please tell me what you would do if you were in my position!"

"I took your advice and walked a mile in my subordinate's shoes"

Clear of troubling thoughts, Thiago forwarded his original email to Dylan the next morning. He added the note, "I had sent this earlier. It perhaps missed your attention since you were dealing with our angry customer."

Chatting one-on-one with Solomon, he found that the designer's sister was critically ill. Thiago allowed him to work from home for the next two weeks to be beside his sister.

Over the next few months, Thiago started applying his mom's advice regularly. He no longer felt as stressed. He was also able to effectively use the reverse empathy technique to get stakeholders to see his point of view.

⭐ EXPERT INSIGHTS

Deepa Bhide MBBS, DCH, PMP

Associate Vice President, Cotiviti India Private Limited.

Projects in Canada, India, UK, USA. **Industries:** Education, Healthcare, Information Technology, Life Sciences, Research.

20+ years of rich experience as healthcare domain expert. Volunteer with PMI since 2007.

Across domains, empathy is a critical project success factor. Improved outcomes are achieved by leveraging the ability to understand and acknowledge others' emotional states, sharing their feelings and creating warmth.

In healthcare, patient-perceived physician empathy[1] has a direct and positive correlation to patient care success. Trust and prompt disclosure of concerns, critical factors, increase when patients perceive that the physician understands their problems.

---

[1] The importance of Empathy in Healthcare (http://blog.medicalgps.com/the-importance-of-empathy-in-healthcare).

To deliver results, you need to effectively play a difficult duet. Let's liken the physician to the project manager and the patient to the team. You need emotional detachment to deliver reasoning-based results. Genuine empathy can dilute judgment or decisions. Success depends on arriving at the right balance.

Empathy can indeed make a project manager's role more meaningful, satisfying, and successful!

Isabelle Levavasseur PMP

Project Manager, Orange.

Projects in Côte d'Ivoire, Congo Democratic Republic, Egypt, Germany, Mauritius, Romania, Slovakia, Spain, UK, USA. **Industries:** Automotive, Retail, Telecommunications, Utilities.

24+ years of experience in delivering project success. Deep expertise in project management methodology and best practices. PMI volunteer since 2004. Vice-President of PMI France Chapter.

I was working on a project and went along well with the customer's representative when I realized that, even if we'd agreed on some actions or decisions, sometimes he didn't do anything or went for other options.

It took me some thinking to understand his motives. This person was nearing retirement and didn't want to be put in an awkward position toward his management. Even when thinking differently and having committed toward the team, he would eventually comply with the management position.

Armed with this understanding, I started preparing stronger arguments to share with him and his management. This proactive approach delivered great results and helped keep the team on track to succeed.

KEYS TO SUCCESS

- High-pressure projects often cause stakeholders to vent frustrations and behave indifferently with each other.
- Project managers seem to suffer the most with such behavior from many sides.
- Looking at the situation from the other person's perspective helps to increase understanding, thus reducing stress levels.
- In situations where others refuse to see your point of view, it helps to ask the question, "I see your point of view. What would you do if you were in my situation?"
- Actively promoting empathy among your team members with exciting role plays goes a long way in reducing team conflicts.

46 Don't Keep Minutes and Lose Hours

Dheeraj was in a slightly playful mood before a project review meeting. With some time to kill, he googled for funny quotes on meetings. Reading John Kenneth Galbraith's quote, "Meetings are indispensable when you don't want to do anything," he smiled.

For project managers, meetings with stakeholders and the team are the lifeline. Meetings happen through a variety of mediums: Across the table in a room, through audio or video (conference calls), and so on. Unproductive meetings can cause project teams hours of lost productivity. For Dheeraj, some meetings were productive and some were exercises in futility.

Dheeraj was heading a prestigious project to build an office complex in the center of the city. One by one, meeting participants walked in. Much to Dheeraj's disappointment, the meeting ended on a sour note. Architect Daniella and scheduler Kevin had veered completely off-topic, fighting over elements of the project's schedule. Discussions on some important drawings ended up only half done. Planning on-site workforce mobilization did not occur at all. With the clock showing an elapsed time of 60 minutes, everyone left. Dheeraj had always set a firm rule that no meeting would continue beyond the allotted time.

Back in his cabin, he began making a note of all the factors that could derail meetings: weak agendas, unprepared participants, discussions that moved away from the agenda, those dominated by a few team members, distractions of smartphones, tablets, and notebook computers, and so on.

Being an analytical person, Dheeraj went through his previous five project review meetings and scored them. Discussions veering away from the agenda was the common problem, followed by poor agendas. In some meetings, distracted participants took to smartphones and laptops.

He found Patrick Lencioni's leadership parable *Death by Meeting* through a Google search. After reading the blurb, he was determined to learn the unconventional approach to solving the meeting problem.

A summary of the book said, "Constructive conflict occurs only when subjects of impact are addressed and debated, allowing for varying opinions and perspectives to be expressed." Patrick explained in the book that a 30-second TV commercial, a one-hour serial episode, and a two-hour movie could not all use the same communication strategy. Likewise, projects suffered due to poor choice of meeting format. Daily check-in meetings had to be short and focused on immediate information sharing. Weekly tactical and monthly strategic meetings had to focus on solutions to pressing problems, avoiding the mere exchange of information. Quarterly and annual strategy meetings would be off-site and feature high-level brainstorming with no set agenda.

Dheeraj also found Dana Brownlee's BLISS strategy in her 2008 PMI Global Congress paper[1], "The Secret to Running Project Status Meetings that Work." BLISS was an

---

[1] https://www.pmi.org/learning/library/secrets-running-project-status-meetings-7009

acronym for: **B**e Efficient, **L**ook Back - Look Forward, **I**nsist on Accountability, **S**implify the Agenda, **S**tay Focused.

In summary, the author had said that efficiency was ensured by effective agendas, time keeping, short meetings, and using a round-robin format to avoid domination. The focus had to be the latest events and highlighting of important immediate milestones. Meeting attendees had to be assigned ownership to specific items and offenders shortlisted. It also helped to stay focused, with a predetermined moderator flagging off-topic discussion, time boxing agenda items, and postponing non-urgent issues.

"We like to spend time on meeting deadlines
rather than on deadly meetings."

Dheeraj now had a big-picture view of meetings from Lencioni's book and on-the-ground input from the BLISS strategy. He set about confidently for his next meeting.

He was sure that his project's meetings would avoid losing valuable hours of productive team time.

EXPERT INSIGHTS

Manga Anantatmula

Controller at Connected Logistics.

Projects in Europe, Pacific, South-West Asia, US Forces Korea, USA. **Industry:** Military.

Over 18 years of experience in project management. Held several key positions in the PM arena, gaining a 360-degree perspective. Currently working as a contracting Acquisition Subject Matter Expert and Team Lead for the US Army.

Meetings must focus on achieving positive outcomes that can lead to better results. A positive tone can be set by starting a meeting with a success story and by acknowledging contributions. The meeting chair should facilitate effective discussions and make it a point to acknowledge good ideas.

It is imperative to be cognizant of existing and potential conflicts, conflicts of interest, protocol, and chain of command while conducting the meeting. Defining meeting etiquette, such as mutual respect, demeanor, and avoiding smartphone distractions are essential for a productive and positive outcome.

Roberto Toledo MBA, PMP

CEO and Founder of Alpha Consultoria, one of Latin America's leading project management training and consulting firms.

Projects in Argentina, Belize, Brazil, Canada, Chile, Colombia, Costa Rica, Dominican Republic, Guatemala, Mexico, Panama, Peru, Poland, UAE, USA, Venezuela. **Industries:** Consulting, Construction, Consumer Products, Education, Engineering, Food and Beverage, Information Technology, Oil and Gas, Pharmaceuticals, Retail, Telecommunications.

Project Management and Strategy Execution professor at Mexico's Institute of Technology (ITAM) and the Inter-American Development Bank (IADB). A PMI volunteer for more than 12 years, currently serving on the PMI Board of Directors (2017–19).

Meetings to present status updates to project sponsors are invaluable in obtaining much-needed support. I recently developed "Roberto's Rules,", a set of proven, practical advice to make these meetings effective:

- *Present relevant data on past events and the current situation candidly and truthfully.*

- *Communicate data on time, cost, scope, resources, risks, and issues plus information which presents the true situation; good or bad.*

- *Use this framework, to focus your message on what lies ahead.*

- *When presenting good news, do not brag. Rather, make it clear that things are going well.*

- *If the news is bad, make sure you recommend a set of viable solutions or corrective actions. If corrective actions are out of your reach, clearly state what you need from the sponsor. Asking for help is not a sign of weakness!*

- *If there is no way to recover the baselined plan, clearly detail the implications for the time, cost and scope objectives of the project.*

KEYS TO SUCCESS

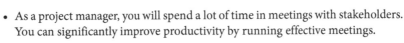
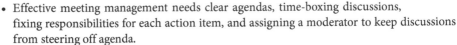

- As a project manager, you will spend a lot of time in meetings with stakeholders. You can significantly improve productivity by running effective meetings.

- Effective meeting management needs clear agendas, time-boxing discussions, fixing responsibilities for each action item, and assigning a moderator to keep discussions from steering off agenda.

- Patrick Lencioni's book *Death by Meeting* provides more details on choosing the right meeting format.

- Adopting the style of agile of stand-up meetings will help you make waterfall information exchange meetings more productive.

Great Catches!

It was Friday evening. Peter was relieved that a terrible work week was behind him.

As the weekend came, his friend Gokul's WhatsApp message made Peter smile: "How about a few games of bowling at this new place, 'Bowled Over'? Their inaugural offer is awesome!" Peter gladly accepted the offer.

As the two friends drove to 'Bowled Over,' Gokul asked, "What's happening, buddy? You look utterly fatigued!"

Peter was surprised how Gokul had read his mind. He responded: "I feel depressed. I recently overheard two team members saying that I was the most negative project manager they'd seen! Is that fair?"

Gokul patted Peter on his shoulder in a reassuring manner. "Calm down bud. Did you think about why they felt that way? Did you get similar feedback in the past?"

That set Peter thinking. After a few seconds, he told Gokul that a common point in the feedback that his managers had given him was that he needed to be more positive with his team members.

He shared a recent incident. Upset by his boss's criticism of project progress, he had gone to the cafeteria to calm down with a cup of coffee. Two of his team members were on a break. Their deliverables were already late by a week. Without a thought, he lashed out at them for "cooling off" in the cafeteria.

Visualizing the situation, Gokul said, "You seem to have let your frustration with the boss spill over onto your team members. It's quite natural. But do you also praise your team members for doing a good job?"

Peter responded. "Not enough. I criticize far, far more than I praise."

It was now Gokul's turn to share a memory: "A leadership workshop I attended featured an eye-opening activity. Rahul, our facilitator, asked us to look around the room to find all things red. Attendees were given a minute to make a mental note of every object of that color and to remember them. The winner of the activity would get a prize. We were then asked to close our eyes. Every attendee was confident of winning by listing most red objects."

Rahul had then said, "Don't open your eyes. List all things green in the room."

The attendees were baffled. In unison, they asked, "Green? Are you kidding? You asked us to look for everything red!"

Rahul had been firm. He had wanted attendees to name all things green in the room. Excepting two attendees, none could name a single item.

Gokul now told Peter, "We learned that this is what we regularly do in our projects. We keep looking for mistakes our team members make. If you keep looking for everything red, you will miss most things green.

"We certainly need to help our colleagues grow by assisting them in tackling their weaknesses and avoiding serious mistakes. However, focusing too much on the negatives can make us blind to all the good things achieved by team members."

Gokul encouraged Peter to deliberately look for positives in his colleagues' work and be generous with praise.

Adding that old habits die hard, he said, "Force yourself to identify the smallest acts of initiative or achievements of team members. Look past raw data like performance appraisals, metrics, and statistics to measure or assess colleagues."

Gokul ended his advice this way: "I know that you care for your team. This approach is one of the easiest and quickest ways of creating a positive working environment. Try this method. Believe me; you'll achieve magical improvement in team morale!"

"Not a birthday party. These are our 'buoyant balloons' to praise good work and buoy team spirit!"

Peter now realized his folly. He made up his mind to see not only the red in his team members' actions, but actively look for, and openly praise many greens.

EXPERT INSIGHTS

Witold Hendrysiak PMP

Portfolio Manager at Raiffeisen Bank Polska S. A. (Raiffeisen Polbank).

Projects in Austria, Poland. **Industry:** Banking.

PMI volunteer since 2003. President, PMI Poland Chapter, (2012–14).

Never underestimate the value of praise. Early in my career, I focused too much on timely delivery of high-quality deliverables. This approach forced me to concentrate on the negatives, causing stress, and drop in team morale levels.

Over time, I learned that public recognition for good performance is a key factor in keeping team members happy and motivated. When individual motivation levels increase, team spirit improves. Team members are willing to learn and take on new responsibilities. People feel empowered when they are allowed to make mistakes. Errors and issues should not be ignored. Rather, project managers should communicate issues and make it clear that mistakes are OK as long as the individual learns from them and does not repeat them.

I achieved amazing results with this approach and you can, too!

Srinivas Maram M.Sc. (E.Eng), M.Ed., PMP

PMP Certification Exam Coach, SMaram Inc; Vice President (Communications), PMI Kazakhstan Potential Chapter.

Projects in Canada, India, Kazakhstan, Russia, USA. **Industries:** Banking, Education, Information Technology, Government.

15+ years of experience in designing business plans, teaching project management courses, strategic business planning, and implementation.

It is an open secret that about 80% of project problems stem from around 20% of project issues. Lack of motivation certainly ranks high in the 20%.

As a project manager, it is easy to fall into the trap of constantly looking for defects in deliverables and team members' performance. While mistakes will certainly need to be analyzed and fixed, focusing too much on the negatives may result in your being tagged as a nitpicker. Your comments may be ignored, upsetting you more. A vicious cycle is now in motion and morale takes a hit!

Make it a habit of catching people doing things right. Compliment them for good work. This approach will motivate team members to contribute more. You have now started a virtuous cycle, which improves team morale and therefore increases the probability of your project's success!

KEYS TO SUCCESS

- As a project manager, you may often find that it is easy to focus on the negatives. After all, errors are common in any project.
- If you focus too much on the errors committed, it is possible that you may miss all the good work that team members are delivering.
- Actively look for positives in team member actions. Compliment them for good performance.
- When you practice this habit mindfully and regularly, you will find that team morale will drastically improve.

48 Critical to Motivation

Brows knitted, head buried in his hands, Mike, the project manager, replayed the past few project team meetings in his mind.

Extremely enthusiastic and energetic when they joined the project a few months back, four members of his team, Siddharth, Justin, Ismail, and Sanjana, now seemed dispirited. The noticeable drop in their motivation levels was starting to affect the whole team. Mike was indeed worried.

He asked himself, "Is there a reason behind this lack of motivation? Did I say or do anything to dent their morale?"

Deep in thought, it suddenly struck him that reduction in drive seemed to have set in after project roles were assigned.

Siddharth and Justin would write large parts of the user manual. Ismail and Sanjana were assigned to carry out unit testing. In past projects, these team members had played the roles of interface designers, database administrators, and programmers. Since the quartet had joined a few months after the project started, Mike had been forced to assign them the roles that remained. He had explained to them that he had no choice, and had promised to assign them the roles they would enjoy as opportunities arose. It now seemed to Mike that they continued to feel that the tasks assigned to them were "boring" and "unimportant."

Dale Carnegie's bestseller, *How to Win Friends and Influence People,* stresses on how almost all individuals crave for respect and importance. Many prefer challenging roles that can bring visibility.

Could Mike abruptly reassign these team members to more visible tasks such as design or development? What would then happen to testing and technical writing?

I was in their path!

But you see, it was at least the critical path!

The project manager browsed through the project schedule. The unit testing tasks were on the project's critical path. If these were delayed, delivery dates for the whole module would slip!

Mike called a meeting with Sanjana and Ismail.

He said, "Guys, I was very impressed with how enthusiastic you were when you joined our project. Your energy levels were incredible. But of late, your participation at meetings has been subdued. I'm worried. Is there anything I can do to help?"

Sanjana opened up: "You know, Mike… The work we're doing is quite repetitive and gets pretty annoying. It's tough to feel excited about what we're doing."

Mike thought about this for a while and said, "At the start of my career I too have been in similar situations. If I were assigned a seemingly unimportant task such as unit testing, my motivation levels would also drop.

"But remember this. This unit testing task lies on our project's critical path. If you don't complete in two weeks, our user manual will get delayed. We'll suffer embarrassment with our customer."

Mike sensed a slight change in the team's mood. He added, "What you are working on is critical to our project. Is someone not giving you the required information? Do you face problems accessing a relevant file?

"My door is always open. I'm willing to spend as much time as you need. Don't hesitate to reach me anytime for anything you need.

"Together, we'll clear all hurdles. Together, let's ensure project success!"

After this conversation, there was a perceptible change in Ismail and Sanjana's demeanor. They looked charged up. The duo walked out of the room seemingly feeling almost half a foot taller!

Mike felt far better now. He actively started thinking of ways to motivate Siddharth and Justin too.

⚙ EXPERT INSIGHTS

Ramam Atmakuri M.Sc., PMP

Executive Vice Chair, L V Prasad Eye Institute. Formerly Vice President, Cognizant Technology Solutions.

Projects in India, UK, USA. **Industries:** Entertainment, Healthcare, Information Technology, Life Sciences, Media.

33+ years. Project, program, and portfolio management leader with a proven track record of delivering project success. Vice President and Center Head for Cognizant, responsible for Hyderabad operations (2010–14). Volunteer with the Project Management Institute (PMI) since 2000. Founder member of the PMI Pearl City Chapter. Served in several global roles with PMI for over a decade: Region Mentor for the South Asia region, Chapter Member Advisory Group, Technology Member Advisory Group. Winner of PMI's prestigious global Eric Jenett Project Management Excellence Award (2012).

To succeed, you need to keep team members on a high – a motivational high! Leveraging the critical path is a great option.

I've used another useful technique: Being proactive in ensuring team members understand their contributions and relate them to the project's big picture goals.

The best product can fail due to poor quality, even when loaded with user-friendly functionality. A poorly written user manual prevents users from deriving full value. The project's testing and technical writing teams do play a significant role.

Motivation levels are boosted when team members understand the criticality of their roles. This approach maximizes the probability of project success.

Margareth F Santos Carneiro MSc, PMP

Owner, PMA - Professional Management.

Projects in Brazil, Canada, Chile, USA. **Industries:** Financial Services, Government.

30+ years experience in governance, project, program and portfolio management, with a proven track record of delivering project success. Volunteer leader with the Project Management Institute (PMI) since 1999. Currently a director of the PMI Board of Directors, (2014–19). Authored a book and co-authored three others. Winner of the PMI GovSIG member of the Year (2003), PMI Distinguished Award (2003), PMI Leadership of the Year (2007), and named one of the world's 25 Most Influential Women in Project Management (2005).

On many projects, I have seen team members get demotivated for various reasons.

Visualizing success is a powerful technique to keep the team motivated. A leader must continually work to share a vision of how the project's success will look like. Make people understand how important their work and deliverables are to project success.

"Hey, the manual you are writing will be used by thousands of users!" "This task of testing is on the project's critical path. If done poorly, our product's quality will be compromised, we will miss milestones, and our project could fail! Your work is crucial to project success!"

Praise team members publicly for good work. Give them visibility and the chance to shine. Recognize contributions. These are essential steps for everyone in the team, but especially for those who are demotivated. Your success depends on the success of your team. Project success is everyone's success.

KEYS TO SUCCESS

- Maintain high levels of motivation to increase productivity and therefore the probability of project success.
- Some project tasks may involve repetitive and seemingly uninteresting activities. Team members assigned to such tasks may feel demotivated since they may think their contribution to the project is unimportant.
- As a project manager, you should reinforce that all tasks contribute to your project's successful completion.
- Where these activities are on the critical path, you should point this out to make the dispirited understand the true importance of their tasks.
- Remember that such proactive actions can significantly boost motivation.

Minor Changes, Major Disaster

Dominic's "Author Genie" project for Selfie Publishing was progressing well.

Late in the afternoon on a Tuesday, he was surprised to see an urgent non-routine meeting invite from Martin, a client representative. Weekly calls usually happened on Fridays, but the new request was for an urgent call on a Wednesday. Martin started with lavish praise for the work Mike's team had put in so far. He then added that he wanted to include "minor" new functionality to the "author sample" web page.

Martin said, "We already provide an option for the authors to design samples themselves. If they feed in some text, our web form will display a sample feel of the page in the chosen format and font. My team has suggested that we add five more fonts to the drop-down."

Dom felt that the addition would not cause too much extra effort, but asked for a change request (CR) from Selfie. As the modification was minor, Martin felt a change request form was not required and that there should be no extra charge. Dom reluctantly agreed.

Tristan, the programmer who was handling author pages, was asked to make the changes. The modification worked perfectly.

The next week, Martin requested the addition of five more fonts, again at no extra charge. Dom asked for a change request. The customer response was that minor changes did not deserve CRs. The team carried out the required modifications.

After Dom delivered the author sample generation module, Selfie's testing team reported regression errors which were causing display of erroneous page counts and hence inaccurate projections of book production cost. The manual versus software estimates differed by as much as 30%.

Dom's team had not foreseen the issue. Every sample font had three options for font and line spacing: 9 on 11 (1.22 line spacing), 10 on 12 (1.20 line spacing), and 11 on 13 (1.18). For each option, the word count per page changed. The seemingly simple action of changing a font could potentially cause a change in word count, and a resultant modification in book production cost. The development team had not considered this complexity.

Jennifer, Dom's boss, called him for an update on the feedback from Selfie. Dom explained the problem and the unrecorded change requests.

Jennifer narrated a story she had heard as an example of how scope creep could occur.

"A man in Alaska had to travel to a nearby town. It would take slightly under two days by dog sled, with no towns on the way. The man packed meat and water for himself and his Huskies for exactly two days. A few hours into his trip, the man noticed a wolf persistently following his sled. 'Maybe it is hungry and smells the meat,' thought the man, pitying the wolf. 'If I throw a small piece of meat, it will go away.'

"How wrong he was! An hour later, the man and his dogs were attacked and severely wounded by a fierce pack of wolves!"

Dom realized that the trickle of change requests he had accepted at the beginning had turned into a flood that could cause a significant delay in his project.

He resolved to push customers to justify the rationale behind every change. Where the changes did not add tangible value, he would push back on the modifications. Where he accepted change, he would negotiate reasonable additional payment. A written change request would be a must.

This sensible approach would prevent the customer from getting habituated to easily getting their way.

Dom would also refer the change requests to the change control board for its overall impact on the project benefits.

The extra work on fonts took three additional weeks as a lot of rework was needed on other modules as well. Dominic was grateful for Jennifer's advice since it helped get the project back on track.

 EXPERT INSIGHTS

Sumanth Padival CSM, PMP

Head of India Operations, SpiderLogic India Pvt. Ltd.

Projects in Australia, Brazil. Germany, India, Singapore, USA. **Industries:** Banking, Insurance, Real Estate.

24 years of experience in IT project and program management. Former volunteer member of the PMI Bangalore India Chapter's Board of Directors. PMI volunteer and former member of the board of PMI Bangalore India Chapter.

Project managers (PMs) often consider accepting requests for changes without regard to the impact of these changes on all stakeholders. The PM therefore unintentionally ends up becoming the primary contributor to the failure of the project. This frequently happens when the PM is self-focused. Examples of self-focus are:

Trying to prove that she/he is a quick decision-maker and hence better than other PMs.

Worrying about the (non-existent?) consequences of saying "No," coupled with the desire to be seen as a considerate PM.

A good PM will always focus her/his efforts on the needs, goals, burdens, challenges, and expectations of the customer, organization, peers, and the team. It is indeed a fine-balancing act. Consistently pulling it off is what makes a PM best at the job!

Alankar Karpe PMP, PMI-ACP

Senior Program Manager, Altisource Labs.

Projects in Australia, Canada, Finland, France, Japan, Malaysia, Singapore, Sweden, USA. **Industries:** Business Consulting, Information Technology.

15+ years of overall experience in program and project management, business analysis, service delivery, strategic business consulting, and market research. Member of PMI's volunteer Ethics Member Advisory Group (2013–2018).

Have you ever delivered a project where no change is requested? Probably not!

In one of my projects, my client asked my team to incorporate a seemingly small change during the development phase. I insisted on a signed change request form. It was submitted after a long delay. We realized during the initial product demo that the client's proposed change would require a significant increase in scope which would cost well over $500,000. The client reluctantly agreed to the increased cost since the added functionality was critical to the solution. I shudder to think what would have happened if I had not insisted on documentation and approval of the change!

KEYS TO SUCCESS

- Controlling scope creep is critical to increasing probability of project success.
- Effectively managing customer requests will help you control scope creep.
- If you accept many seemingly minor requests for free changes early in the project, you will convey the impression that you are open to much more. Scope creep will then quickly turn unmanageable.
- Resist the temptation to accept requests for change blindly or with no constructive discussion. Ask customers to provide a detailed rationale for each change. Unless the change is well-justified and will be paid for, politely refuse even seemingly simple changes.
- Where changes are accepted, insist on documentation of the changes through formal Change Requests (CRs). To ensure all impacts of change are considered, have the CRs processed through the Change Control Board.

50   Chase Them Down

Dheeraj's appointment as a consultant project manager to implement a facility management solution for Galaxy Infra was yet another milestone in his career. The project involved customizing and implementing FMWare, an off-the-shelf software product from FalconEye.

Sipping his favorite green tea, Dheeraj was both excited and anxious. He was determined to do everything possible to ensure success. This project would showcase his ability to customize off-the-shelf products.

FalconEye's team had been hard at work customizing FMWare to match Galaxy's requirements for over six months. Final user acceptance testing was just weeks away. The proactive PM that he always was, Dheeraj had arranged fortnightly sessions for users to play around with customizations. He was sure that this approach would help his team gather regular feedback.

In one of these early sessions four months back, Marty, an experienced user, suggested adding floor number and room type information to a work order report. He had said that this addition would ease the work of facilities personnel. As this seemed to be an easy fix, FalconEye readily agreed to make the change.

In another session, Élise a key stakeholder, found a defect that could seriously affect usability: Work order types in a drop-down field were listed in random order rather than alphabetically. The requirements document clearly specified that all drop-down fields displayed items in alphabetical order. Dheeraj's team members noted down this defect and promised to communicate it to FalconEye.

Three months down the line, Marty and Élise were testing other new features. They noticed that their valid concerns were still unimplemented.

A worried Marty said, "You said this was an easy fix. You told me FalconEye would get this done. It's now 12 weeks. What's the point in getting my feedback if you don't act on them? If this trend continues, I'll have no option but to escalate the issue to my boss."

Élise expressed similar sentiments. Other users doubted if their suggestions were taken seriously.

Dheeraj apologized to his users. He promised to investigate and rectify the problem. On checking with his team, he found that FalconEye had missed implementing Marty's suggestion. For Élise's idea, his team had forgotten to communicate to the vendor.

Dheeraj realized that this situation could soon turn dangerous. He consulted Yury, one of the top project management experts in the city.

On analyzing the situation, Yury said that the root cause of the team's challenges lay in ineffective issue tracking. Quoting the oft-repeated truism, "A stitch in time saves nine," he suggested a set of effective steps to prevent recurrences:

1. Create and staff the role of "Issue Manager." This person's full-time role is to chase every issue to resolution. When faced with serious hurdles, they have the authority to escalate.

2. Promptly document every issue, technical or functional, in the project's Issue Register.

3. Determine a priority, "Low," "Medium," or "High" represented by the numbers 1, 2, or 3. Alternatively, use 5-point or 10-point scales.

4. Document each issue's date. Add the computed column "Ageing," which displays the number of days each issue has remained open.

5. Issue Managers measure their effectiveness by how many issues they can expeditiously close, not just those that are of high priority.

6. They can spot patterns and trends in issues. This information is valuable in avoiding future issues.

Dheeraj realized the immense value of these suggestions.

Implementing them brought excellent results. His team regained the trust of Marty, Élise, and other key stakeholders.

Issue Management was no longer a serious issue for this team!

"Cross off issues to keep Issue Count Dracula at bay"

 ## EXPERT INSIGHTS

Kannan Ganesan MA, MBA, MCA, MS, CAIIB, PMP

Senior Director - Software Development & Delivery, FIS Global Business Solutions India Pvt. Ltd.

Projects in Australia, Brazil, Canada, Peru, Saudi Arabia, Singapore, Thailand, UAE, USA, Vietnam. **Industries:** Banking and Financial Services.

34+ years in managing IT projects. Deep expertise in delivery of global captive application service projects for an international banking technology solutions organization. As a PMI volunteer, served in several roles for 15+ years: Founder Board member of the PMI Chennai Chapter, Leadership Institute Advisory Group, Virtual Community Advisory Group, and Community of Practice Member Advisory Group.

I achieved successful and consistent delivery from offshore by adopting a proactive attitude toward managing issues. Timely fixes save considerable time and money. Where serious issues cannot be closed swiftly, it is critical to assign team members the responsibility to track to closure by helping remove hurdles. Else, the issues can rapidly grow in seriousness to the point where they threaten the entire project! To summarize:

- *Acknowledge issues and communicate them clearly.*
- *Set reasonable expectations about issue resolution.*
- *Assign team members the right levels of authority and responsibility to tackle issues.*
- *Encourage the team to find smart and innovative solutions.*
- *Escalate serious issues to the right level of management.*

Markus Klein PMP

Projects in Germany, USA. **Industries:** Financial Services, Retail.

17+ years in IT outsourcing, IT for financial institutes; ERP, strategy implementation. creating PMOs, delivery, governance and change management. PMI volunteer for several years. Social Media Expert for project management and founder of www.projectmanagement.plus; www.pmcertification-online.de and creator of "MP4PM – MindmaPping for Project Management."

I firmly believe that issue management does not get the importance that it deserves. I am of the opinion that this area should be accorded as much priority as risk management. After all, these two processes are closely interrelated: Identified issues can result in new risks. A risk, when not effectively managed, can become a real issue.

A proven project management best practice is to create the specific role of "Issue Manager" and implement a process to assign a priority rating and owners for every issue. For priorities, I recommend using even numbers (2, 4, 6, and so on) to avoid the tendency to the mean.

The issue manager communicates on a regular basis with issue owners. He or she is given the mandate to track issues to closure and escalate to higher levels wherever necessary.

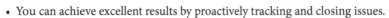

KEYS TO SUCCESS

- You can achieve excellent results by proactively tracking and closing issues.
- Since your team may often grapple with time constraints, it is entirely possible for minor issues to be overlooked.
- By systematically tracking all issues to closure, your team can avoid the risk of small issues becoming major problems.
- Appoint a team member to the full-time position of "Issue Manager" with the mandate to document, track, and chase all issues to closure.
- For every entry in the Issue Log, determine issue priorities and the number of days every issue has been open. This information is invaluable in quickly resolving issues.

Let's Cut Cake!

Paresh said, "What a boring meeting!" Alisha added, "All we do is talk about work and upcoming modules like we're a bunch of machines." Project manager Mike walked by as these comments were being aired. Unaware of his presence, his colleagues were chatting about the previous day's meeting.

Mike was straight-jacketed and laser-focused on upcoming project tasks or the next phase of his project. His meeting agendas focused on discussing the future rather than the past, and he often stated, "Previous achievements have been done and dusted. We move on."

This attitude did not go down well with the team.

On Sunday, Mike was having lunch with his father Robert, a recently retired CEO of a mid-sized firm. Rob was always generous with well-meaning advice to anyone who approached him.

"Dad, I'm frustrated! I treat my team well. I meet them frequently to discuss what's coming next. Look at how they repay me. With snide comments behind my back!"

Rob listened patiently to his son's rant. Knowing Mike's future focus well, he asked, "Son, it looks like your team members are frustrated too. Do you appreciate their work? Do you celebrate project achievements?"

"I do give them the occasional pat on the back. I send regular appreciation emails to my colleagues, giving them visibility by marking copies to my boss. Isn't this enough?"

Mike's dad smiled. "Occasional pats on the back and appreciation emails just won't do. You need to do much more. Human beings feel great when they are congratulated for their small wins. Some believe it doesn't pay to keep looking in the rearview mirror. There's no harm in looking back. However, I always made it a point to organize impromptu celebrations on completing every milestone. I found ways to highlight positives even when a project was not going well. Let me get you something I recently read."

Mission accomplished!

Yippee!! Let's order pizza to celebrate!!! And for you out there, which address should we order delivery?

Rob gave Mike a print-out of an *Inc.* magazine article titled "Why You Must Celebrate Small Successes." He had highlighted some text in green. It read: "To succeed in a big endeavor, you must 'parcel the journey out into the smaller steps you'll take along the way' and 'celebrate when you reach one.'"[1]

He added, "The principle also applies to project completion. We're not robots. We need to celebrate to recharge for

---

[1] https://www.inc.com/minda-zetlin/why-you-must-celebrate-small-successes.html

the next project. You can set aside a budget for bigger project-end celebrations. You should get your team members to share their success stories, turning points, and even funny moments. Try ordering inexpensive mementos for everyone, something they can remember the project by!"

Mike had learnt a lot from his father's practical advice. As a first step, he changed his team meeting agenda to start with "Weekly Wins." A five-minute slot on the agenda was allotted for team members to share recent accomplishments. Then, the team would discuss activities due in the coming week.

An impromptu pizza meeting greeted team members on completing the project's next milestone. Taking a cue from Mike, team leads organized similar celebrations on team achievements.

Mike was on the way to the pantry to get his third caffeine fix of the day. He overheard Paresh say, "What a sudden change in our meetings! I wonder if some angel advised Mike in his dream."

Mike smiled. He knew the angels who helped him change were his dad, Paresh, and Alisha!

EXPERT INSIGHTS

Ricardo Triana PMP, Prince2

CEO and President, Practical Thinking Group and Project Management Advisor, United Nations Office of Project Services (UNOPS).

Projects in Argentina, Australia, Brazil, Chile, Colombia, Ireland, Mexico, Netherlands, Niger, Peru, Singapore, Spain, USA, Venezuela, Zambia. **Industries:** Development Projects, Financial Services, Infrastructure, Information Technology, Mining, Telecommunications.

A seasoned professional with 20+ years of professional experience. Recognized international speaker and consultant with specialization in leadership, conflict management, strategy, and organizational project management. Member of the PMI Global Board of Directors (2010–15). Chairman of the PMI Board (2014).

Almost all of my professional experience has been in rescuing troubled projects. I learned that, most of the time, the reasons for failure are not technical. Rather, they are interpersonal.

The team's perception of how a project is progressing toward the future is paramount. You don't have to wait until the project has ended to celebrate and run. Celebrate small milestones while we learn from our achievements and mistakes. This approach creates a ripple effect in the team and will allow you to keep them engaged and optimistic even during tough times. In the end, optimism and engagement are for free. There's no need to get anything from the project budget!

Aruni Siriwardene M.Sc., PgDip BA, PMP

Projects in Australia, Bangladesh, Canada, Malaysia, Sri Lanka, UK, USA. **Industries:** Apparel, Fashion, Financial Services, Food and Beverages, Government, Healthcare, Manufacturing.

21+ years of experience in enterprise resource planning, software development life cycle, strategy planning and implementation. Strong expertise in risk management, execution excellence, governance, revenue and budget management. Volunteer with PMI for many years, including the role of Director (Communications) with the PMI Colombo Chapter (2009–10). Long-time Rotarian. President of the Rotary Club of Colombo Regency (2017–18).

People learn more by hearing a happy story of success than from numerous stories of lessons learned to focus on wrongs!

"Once upon a time, a dedicated team toiled hard to complete a difficult project. Many, varied challenges that manifested were courageously thwarted. The secret to this courage was that much was spoken of and celebrated about every success they achieved. Simple stories, meaningful modest, genuine celebrations carrying the message of appreciation.

"The team achieved success; gained confidence and pride, and went on to repeat success. What of failures?! Addressed, but quietly."

Celebrate today's success today; because tomorrow might bring more!

KEYS TO SUCCESS

- As a project manager, you would have noticed that teams often rush to the next project without pausing to stop and savor the success of the previous effort.

- You will realize that every project, even one that failed, had successes that should be cherished.

- Celebrate successes to help you and your team boost morale and start the next project or phase with higher levels of motivation.

- Don't feel compelled to make the celebrations extensive or expensive. A simple meeting with economical gifts will do.

- Encourage your teams to celebrate important milestones. These celebrations will re-energize the team for the road ahead.

52 Lessons That Matter

Ganesh paced back and forth, lost in thought. Though labeled "Lessons Learned sessions," the previous three project post-mortem meetings had ended in a fracas. Blame games and scapegoating took away most of the time. There was no useful outcome.

Ganesh's primary objectives in conducting those meetings were to discuss major successes, failure factors, and effective documentation to significantly help future projects.

Ganesh's boss Richard referred him to Emilio, a senior manager who was well known for expertly running project post mortem meetings. Emilio shared his six success secrets for great Lessons Learned session:

1. Obtain firm time commitments from key stakeholders: Insights from a wide range of project stakeholders will go a long way toward ensuring an extensive collection of lessons learned.

2. Keep the agenda clear and positive: Team members often have negative perceptions of such meetings. Counter this opinion by designing an agenda that starts with discussing project successes and achievements.

3. Praise the positives: Invite team members to share key project success techniques and accomplishments. While doing so, encourage them to name specific colleagues or teams who enabled the achievements.

4. Potential Improvement Points (PIPs): Next, discuss project challenges, issues, and missteps. Calling this part of the meeting "Potential Improvement Points" helps maintain the positive tone. Invite team members to list as many areas of potential improvement as possible. Focus on collecting a large list of PIPs rather than discussing possible solutions to specific issues.

5. Steer clear of personal attacks: Finger-pointing and finding scapegoats are frequently a big problem in lessons learned sessions. The meeting chairman makes it clear that no naming of individuals or teams will be allowed. Why? People named as being responsible for errors are pushed to the defensive and may stop contributing. Worse, they may retaliate with counter accusations, causing the meeting to descend into a shouting match.

   The focus is on areas where improvements can be made in future projects rather than on finger pointing and assigning blame.

6. Document for easy retrieval: A well-planned and effectively run Lessons Learned session yields a treasure trove of repeatable actions that brought success and the many missteps that can be avoided. Project managers will need to document these items in detail.

   Emilio added that it was not enough to merely document the Lessons Learned and file them away in a difficult-to-access archive. Rather, they had to be stored in a keyword-searchable database with appropriate access security. This database would be invaluable when planning new projects.

After carefully listening to Emilio, Ganesh set up an agenda for his next Lessons Learned session. He set the tone for the meeting by congratulating the team on successful completion of the project and asked each team member for insights. As the positives lifted the morale of the team, Ganesh gently asked each member what could be done differently in the next project to avoid missteps. Potential improvement points were documented, and Ganesh asked the team to keep them in mind when the next project was planned. Each team member left the meeting smiling.

Ganesh made it a point to spend the next hour documenting the lessons learned and uploading them into the project knowledge database.

He too smiled. In the end, these lessons would help many projects succeed!

"Yes, daddy has homework too...he is preparing
his 'lessons learned' document"

EXPERT INSIGHTS

Miroslav Anicin MScEE, PMP, PMI-ACP, PMI-PBA, CBAP, PSM, CSM, CSPO

Agile PMO and Agile Digital Transformation Consultant, Squaring the Project, Serbia.

Projects in Bosnia and Herzegovina, Montenegro, Serbia, Sweden, UK. **Industries:** Financial Services, FMCG, Hospitality, Public, Telecommunications.

25+ years of experience in organizational agile transformation, strategic business consulting, project management, rescuing projects from crisis, business analysis, and business process management. President, PMI Serbia Chapter.

We think of Lessons Learned (LLs) mostly in the light of valuable contribution for future projects. Thus, we are collecting them at the end of projects. My experience is that LL's need to be collected along the project lifecycle, along the lines of agile retrospectives. When collecting LLs, it is crucial to communicate clearly that the primary purpose of the LL session is to find potential improvement points (PIPs); the intention is certainly not to assign blame or find scapegoats.

This approach has two significant advantages:

a. *Documenting PIPs immediately eliminates the chance that they are forgotten at the end of the project lessons learned session.*

b. *We can avoid repetition of the same errors in the later phases of the same project.*

Shaligram Pokharel PhD

Professor of Industrial and Systems Engineering at Qatar University.

Projects in Nepal, Qatar, Singapore, USA. **Industries:** Education and Energy.

First Honorary Secretary of PMI Singapore Chapter. Over nine years as PMI global volunteer in a variety of roles including Region Mentor and on the Chapter Member Advisory Group.

To err is human. However, repeatedly committing the same mistakes is a sure path to project failure.

As a veteran project manager, faculty and Region Mentor with the Project Management Institute, I have benefited much from lessons learned sessions and databases. I make it a priority to communicate their importance at every opportunity.

Every project, whether it is small, medium or large, whether it is commercial or not-for-profit, can benefit from effective lessons learned sessions.

When PMI chapters conducted effective lessons learned sessions, leaders benefited immensely by understanding the importance of managing ethnocultural values and allotting volunteers to tasks in their areas of expertise and passion. Chapter leaders also realized that large buffers are a must in volunteer projects since people have other important priorities.

KEYS TO SUCCESS

- Lessons learned sessions play a critical role in helping you document learning which can be invaluable in future projects or phases.

- Conduct these sessions frequently. They are not meant to be carried out only at the end of the project.

- Invite all key stakeholders to the meeting. Their inputs will increase the depth of discussions.

- Since such sessions are typically considered to be exercises in finger pointing and assigning blame, you should make every effort to set a positive tone.

- Start with the positives. Discuss successful techniques and innovations which can be repeated in future project or phases. Name the people and teams responsible for these successes.

- Next on the agenda will be "Potential Improvement Points." Make it clear that you will not tolerate naming people or teams. The focus is on issues, not individuals. Discuss things that can be done better in the future.

- Make sure all learnings are collated and stored in your organization's keyword-searchable database for reference in future projects.

Appendices

Top Failure Factors Linked with Practical Solutions

The table below lists the top factors causing project failure, ranked in descending order. This list is a critical part of our learning that we share with you. It helps you choose what to read first.

Identify your biggest pain points and read the corresponding primary chapters. Once you are done, move to the supporting chapters.

For example, if fuzzy scope and scope creep are your biggest challenges, select factors numbers six and two. Start by reading the chapters in the "Primary Chapter(s)" column. In this case, you will first read chapters 10, 14, 19 and 20. Next read the chapters in the column, "Supporting Chapter(s)."

Next move on to your other challenges and so on.

#	Failure Factor	Primary Chapter(s)	Supporting Chapter(s)
1	Inadequate or Improper Planning	15, 17	8, 9, 52
2	Fuzzy or Missing Requirements	10, 20	8, 14, 19, 49
3	Unrealistic Stakeholder Expectations	4	12, 14, 23, 46
4	Lack of Senior Management Engagement	2, 3	1, 18, 31
5	Unclear or Inadequate Communication	6	26, 33, 36, 39, 46. 50
6	Ineffective Scope Management & Scope Creep	10, 14, 19	22, 49, 52
7	Lack of Alignment to Organizational Goals	3	2, 18
8	Ineffective Time and Cost Estimation	27, 31, 32	8
9	Ineffective or Unethical Leadership	1, 3, 13, 29	18, 31, 45, 47
10	Inadequate Stakeholder Engagement	2, 11, 20, 23	1, 4, 6, 7, 12
11	Poor Team Morale	42, 47	24, 38, 41, 44, 48, 51
12	Mismanagement of Change	7, 10, 49, 50	40
13	Ineffective or Poor Risk Management	21, 30, 34, 35, 40	33
14	Skill Gap and Resource Mismatch	43, 9	5
15	Ineffective Schedule Management	32, 37, 40, 48	8, 27, 31
16	Poor or Missing Project Management Skills	13	5, 9, 10, 15, 33

17	Lack of Project Management Methodology	8	13, 15, 16, 24, 28, 31, 47
18	Ineffective Task Assignments	**25, 43**	5, 9
19	Ineffective Procurement	**11, 23**	8, 49
20	Mismanaging Conflicts	**33**	19, 20, 23

Expert Contributors

This book was enriched with valuable insights from 108 project management veterans and experts who have delivered 2000+ successful projects in 119 countries across 54 industries. They deserve kudos for providing insights that enrich your perspective on project management.

#	Expert	Chapter #	#	Expert	Chapter #
1	Acilio Marinello	23	25	Fahad Ahmed	17
2	Adilson Pize	16	26	Farhad Abdollahyan	43
3	Agnieszka Gasperini	39	27	Gary Hamilton	33
4	Alankar Karpe	49	28	Ilango Vasudevan	5
5	Allan Mills	28	29	Imre Szalay	43
6	Altaf Hossain S M	34	30	Isabelle Levavasseur	45
7	Amany Nuseibeh	25	31	Ivo Michalik	5
8	Amitava Banerjee	10	32	Jacob Zachariah	44
9	Ammarah Shahzad	31	33	Jayakrishnan P S	11
10	Archana Raghuram	9	34	Jesse Fewell	8
11	Arun Kiran Ponnekanti	39	35	Joanna Newman	18
12	Aruni Siriwardene	51	36	John Watson	19
13	Barbara Porter	23	37	Julio Carazo	27
14	Brajesh Kaimal	37	38	Kannan Ganesan	50
15	Cecilia Boggi	36	39	Karen Clarke	14
16	Chakradhar Iyyunni	32	40	Karthik Ramamurthy	Author
17	Chandramouli Subramanian	30	41	Koushik Srinivasan	38
18	Chandrasekhara Rao V T	33	42	Kwame Justice	18
19	Chandrasekaran A	1	43	Lily Murariu	16
20	Cristian Soto	24	44	Mahendiran Periyasamy	7
21	Daisy Ruiz Lovera	11	45	Malgorzata Kusyk	40
22	Deepa Bhide	45	46	Manga Anantatmula	46
23	Esteban Villegas	22	47	Margareth Carneiro	48
24	Fabio Rigamonti	6	48	Markus Klein	50

49	Mary Mateja	42		79	Roberto Toledo	46
50	Meera Venkat	28		80	Saravanan Velrajan	36
51	Miguel Cotrina	12		81	Sasi Kumar	29
52	Mike O'Brochta	29		82	Shaligram Pokharel	52
53	Milton Carvajal	21		83	Shinichi Tasaka	15
54	Miroslav Anicin	52		84	Simona Bonghez	41
55	Mohamed Khalifa	37		85	Sivaram Athmakuri	8
56	Mohammad Ashraf Khan	32		86	Sreedharan E	10 Golden Keys
57	Mohammad Ichsan	27		87	Srinivas Maram	47
58	Muhammad Ilyas	12		88	Sripriya Narayanasamy	Author
59	Mustafa Hafizoglu	7		89	Sriram Srinivasan	22
60	Naomi Caietti	13		90	Sukumar Rajagopal	17
61	Olivier Lazar	4		91	Sumanth Padival	49
62	Pablo Lledó	41		92	Sumit Sinha	2
63	Padmaja S N	42		93	Syed Nazir Razik	6
64	Pat Robertson	31		94	Tejas Sura	40
65	Paul Pelletier	13		95	Theofanis Giotis	14
66	Prasanna Sampathkumar	25		96	Thomas George	20
67	Raghuram Sarangan	4		97	Thomas Walenta	2
68	Rahul Sudame	9		98	Upendra Babu	15
69	Raju Rao	24		99	Vadim Bogdanov	17
70	Ramam Atmakuri	48		100	Venkat Ramachandran	3
71	Ramanatha Siva C V	3		101	Venkata Subramanian D	38
72	Rami Kaibni	10		102	Vinay Babu Manepalli	44
73	Randy Black	30		103	Visukumar Gopal	26
74	Ravi Vurakaranam	19		104	Vittal Anantatmula	35
75	Ray Frohnhoefer	34		105	Vittal Raj R	35
76	Rene Heredia	26		106	Witold Hendrysiak	47
77	Ricardo Triana	51		107	Zahara Khan	20
78	Rick Morris	1		108	Zulkhernain Shamsuddin	21

List of Countries

Listed here are the 119 countries where our 108 experts have delivered successful projects. The map at the end of the list shows our book's extensive global coverage.

Afghanistan	Ecuador	Malaysia
Argentina	Egypt	Mauritius
Australia	El Salvador	Mexico
Austria	Estonia	Moldova
Bahrain	Ethiopia	Mongolia
Bangladesh	Finland	Montenegro
Belarus	France	Morocco
Belgium	Germany	Myanmar
Belize	Ghana	Nation of Brunei
Bolivia	Greece	Nepal
Bosnia and Herzegovina	Guatemala	Netherlands
Botswana	Haiti	New Zealand
Brazil	Honduras	Nicaragua
Bulgaria	Hong Kong	Niger
Cambodia	Hungary	Nigeria
Cameroon	India	North Korea
Canada	Indonesia	Norway
Central African Republic	Iran	Oman
Chile	Iraq	Pakistan
China	Ireland	Palestine
Colombia	Italy	Panama
Costa Rica	Japan	Paraguay
Côte d'Ivoire	Jordan	Peru
Croatia	Kazakhstan	Philippines
Cyprus	Kenya	Poland
Czech Republic	Kuwait	Portugal
Denmark including Greenland	Latvia	Puerto Rico
Dominican Republic	Lebanon	Qatar
Dem. Republic of Congo	Lithuania	Republic of Congo

Romania	Sri Lanka	Ukraine
Russia	Sudan	United Arab Emirates
Saudi Arabia	Sweden	United Kingdom
Senegal	Switzerland	United States of America
Serbia	Taiwan	Uruguay
Singapore	Tanzania	Venezuela
Slovakia	Thailand	Vietnam
South Africa	Trinidad and Tobago	Yemen
South Korea	Tunisia	Zambia
South Sudan	Turkey	Zimbabwe
Spain	Uganda	

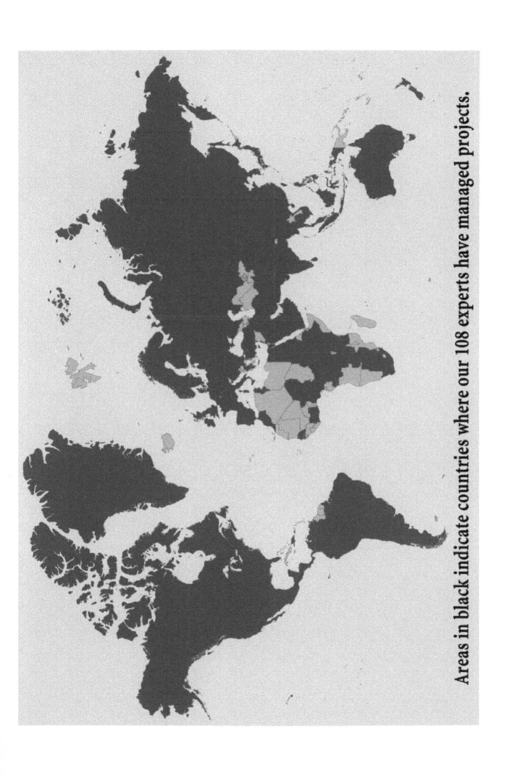

Areas in black indicate countries where our 108 experts have managed projects.

List of Industries

Listed here are the 54 industries where our 108 experts have delivered successful projects. Note: Some industry segments have been combined according to relevance.

Aeronautics & Aerospace	Insurance
Agriculture	IT Enabled Services & BPO
Apparel & Fashion	Law Enforcement
Automobiles	Legal, Law & Justice
Aviation, Shipping & Transportation	Life Sciences
Banking, Finance & Investment	Logistics
Biometrics	Lottery & Gaming
Chemicals	Manufacturing
Communications	Media, Publishing & Entertainment
Construction	Medical Devices
Consulting & Professional Services	Mining & Natural Resources
Consumer Goods	Mobile Applications
Defence	Non-profits
Design	Nuclear Equipment
E-commerce	Petrochemicals
Education & E-Learning	Pharmaceuticals & Medical Devices
Electronics	Postal Services
Energy, Oil & Gas	Procurement
Engineering	Product Development
Food & Beverages	Real Estate
Gifting Services	Relocation
Government	Research & Development
Healthcare	Retail
Hospitality	Supply Chain
Human Resources	Telecommunications
Information Technology	Tourism
Infrastructure	Utilities

Key Contributors

Amber and Arun added excellent value to this book by contributing superb cartoons which add a dash of humor to an otherwise serious subject. Venkatesh made the book so much better with his brilliant suggestions and excellent professional editing.

Amber Marfatia

Firmly believes that cartoons take advantage of an eye's eagerness to find logic in shapes and gags and while doing so, it certainly tickles the funny bone. Also believes that a cartoon is a collaboration between an artist and the reader and a quick vacation from sad, boring reality. His single panel cartoons appear in *Gujarat Daily*, various newsletters, technology sites, and at www.toonstory.in. Feel free to drop him a note on any of these mediums:

www.toonstory.in

www.facebook.com/toonstory.in

www.instagram.com/toonstory.in

Arun Ramkumar

Uses the medium of cartoons and comic strips to express his skewed worldview in the hope of eliciting a chuckle or two from his audience while overlooking his various foibles and eccentricities. His cartoons have featured in *The New Indian Express, The Hindu, Fountain Ink magazine, ESPNCricinfo, Vidura,* and other print/web media publications. His repertoire includes comic strips, gag cartoons, caricatures, editorial cartoons, book illustrations, and logo designs. Feel free to drop him a note on any of these mediums:

www.arun-bohemianwanderer.blogspot.com

www.facebook.com/arun.ramkumar

www.twitter.com/arun_bohemian

Venkatesh Krishnamoorthy

Edits scholarly books for a living, reads a lot of books to make his life better, writes stories about people, places, and events that he feels need to be told. Authored *A Tale of Two Schools*, tracing the journey of two leading Chennai schools run by the Indian Educational Trust. His business VirtualPaper provides a range of editorial services, including value-added language editing to self-publishing authors. Wrote stories about startups, entrepreneurs, funding, and so on for YourStory.com, a leading portal for Indian businessmen. He can be reached at kvenkatesh@virtualpaper.co.in or any of these mediums:

www.facebook.com/krishvenkatesh2011

www.twitter.com/krishvenkatesh

Authors

Karthik Ramamurthy MCA, MBA, PMP

Project, Program & Portfolio Management (P3M), Leadership and Social Media expert with over 30 years of experience delivering project success across many continents. He is a powerful keynote speaker, presenter, moderator, and panelist at several national and international events.

As Founder and Principal Consultant of KeyResultz, Karthik has helped numerous organizations derive positive results by harnessing the power of global project management best practices. His areas of professional expertise include Project Management Offices (PMOs), Risk Management, Facilitated Lessons Learned sessions, and Project Knowledge Bases.

He is a guest faculty at prestigious institutions such as the Indian Institute of Management (IIM), L&T Institute of Project Management, Reserve Bank of India (RBI) Staff College, and Project Management Institute (PMI) chapters. He has trained thousands of professionals in project management best practices, global certifications, and soft skills in hundreds of sessions across industries.

Karthik has served as a volunteer and volunteer leader with PMI since 2005, serving in several local and global roles: Chapter President, Member of the Chapter Excellence Awards Review Committee, and Community Moderator for PMI's LinkedIn group, "PMI Project, Program and Portfolio Management: #1 group for career advancement."

A graduate of the PMI Leadership Institute Master Class (LIMC), he has served on the Ethics Member Advisory Group since 2017.

Karthik's passions include Quizzing, Cricket, Cryptic Crosswords, Reading, and Volunteering. He has been a Quiz Master, Cryptic Crossword Compiler, and writer on cricket for several decades.

You can connect with him at https://www.linkedin.com/in/kramamurthy and follow him on Twitter: @KarthikPMO.

Sripriya Narayanasamy MCA, PMP

Accomplished Project, Program & Portfolio Management (P3M) professional with a 25-year track record of leading project success across Asia, Europe, North America, and South America.

As co-founder of KeyResultz, Priya has helped many organizations achieve project success through her areas of deep expertise: Project Management Office (PMO) set up and optimization, Executive Dashboards, and Project Knowledge Bases.

Priya leverages her bubbly personality by helping teams harness the power of increased morale through Gamification, implementing the Fish philosophy at work, and Appreciation Circles.

Her top five Gallup Strengths: Positivity, Persuader, Maximizer, Communicator, and Arranger.

She is an expert trainer in various project management and soft skills topics. A volunteer with the PMI Chennai Chapter since 2005, she served as Associate Vice President for Certification. She won the 2012 "Volunteer of the Year" award.

Priya's passions include Writing, Music, Reading, Volunteering and Mentoring the next generation to achieve their fullest potential.

You may connect with her at https://www.linkedin.com/in/priyavns and follow her on Twitter: @PriyaPMO.

Project Success Workshops and Consulting

Does your organization get real return on investment (ROI) on your project management consulting and training spends?

KeyResultz can help you boost project success through workshops and consulting services that provide measurable value and therefore increased ROI.

1. **Project Success workshops:** Harnessing the power of the success techniques in the book and our rich experience, we design customized workshops focusing on your biggest pain points.

   Leveraging the power of gamification, case studies, and role plays, we equip your teams with the knowledge and skills required to boost productivity and therefore project success.

   Want to boost your project managers' leadership skills? We can design customized programs on critical topics such as Powerful Presentation, Effective Communication, Writing Winning Proposals, and Win-Win Negotiation.

   Workshops can range from one day to four or more.

   We can also develop custom quizzes and contests that can boost employee engagement and organizational knowledge.

2. **Consulting which focuses on real results:** We have an impressive track record of helping clients harness the power of global project management best practices and the success tips in this book. We can help you in the following areas:

   - Project Management Office (PMO) set-up and optimization
   - Facilitated Risk Management
   - Effective Scope Management
   - Programs to boost Team Morale
   - Facilitated Lessons Learned Sessions
   - Development of Project Knowledge Bases

   To explore more, please email us at marketing@keyresultz.com

Key Project Management Terms in This Book

Say Yes to Project Success was written to help anyone involved in projects, not just project managers. This appendix is intended for readers who may not have had formal training in project management. This book's website, ProjectSuccessBook.com includes a more detailed list of terms.

A much more comprehensive list is available in the Project Management Institute's *Lexicon of Project Management Terms*.[1]

Acceptance Criteria: A set of conditions that the project's product, service, or result is expected to meet before deliverables can be accepted by the client.

Agile Software Development: A time boxed, iterative approach to software delivery. It helps build software incrementally from the start of the project, instead of trying to deliver it all at the end of.

Change Control Board (CCB): A formally constituted expert committee which makes collective decisions on change requests. CCBs are tasked with analyzing all potential impacts of a proposed change and making informed decisions on whether to approve, delay or reject CRs. The CCB then documents and communicates the decisions to relevant stakeholders.

Change Request (CR): A formal proposal for any alteration to project documents, baselines or deliverables. CRs may be submitted by the project team and/or clients for alteration to the project or the product of the project.

Communication Management Plan: A key project document which defines the communication requirements of project stakeholders. It also describes how project information will be distributed and how feedback will be received from stakeholders.

Critical Chain Project Management (CCPM): A scheduling method which focuses on identifying, analyzing, and eliminating or mitigating resource bottlenecks using time and resource buffers. Resources can include people, equipment, physical space, logistics, and so on.

Critical Path (CP): The longest sequence of activities in a project which determines the shortest time in which a project can be completed. The critical path is a key project management tool since any delay in an activity on the critical path can cause delays to the entire project.

Deliverable: Any unique product, service or result which a project was undertaken to produce. Deliverables may be tangible or intangible, and are described in project requirements documents.

---

[1] The Project Management Institute's PMI Lexicon of Project Management Terms v3.1 https://www.pmi.org/pmbok-guide-standards/lexicon

Estimating: A critical part of project planning which involves arriving at quantitative estimates of project costs, durations, or resources.

Gold Plating: The act of giving the client more functionality, features or quality than what was originally agreed upon, without approvals and no additional payment.

Issue log: An important communication and reporting tool which helps project teams record, analyze and track ongoing and closed project issues.

Lessons Learned: Knowledge gained by project managers and project teams from the process of performing their projects. Formal lessons learned sessions are usually conducted close to the completion of a project phase or the entire project.

Milestone: A significant point or event in the project timeline which indicates completion of one or more primary objectives.

Padding: Additional time or cost which project managers or project teams may arbitrarily add to their estimates.

Project Management Plan: A critical project document which describes how the project will be executed, monitored, controlled and closed.[1] It includes subsidiary plans in the areas of scope, schedule, cost, risk, quality, resources, communications, stakeholder, procurement, and so on.

Project Management Office (PMO): A group or department within an organization which defines and maintains project management standards. PMOs help organizations in sharing project management methodologies, best practices, tools, and techniques.

RACI Chart (also called Responsibility Assignment Matrices): A matrix of all the activities matched against individuals or groups of project contributors. At the project level, RACI charts are used to assign project roles or large work packages to specific teams. When created at the team level, these charts help in assigning specific team responsibilities or deliverables to individual team members. R stands for "Responsible," A for "Accountable," C for "Consult" and I for "Inform."

Requirement Traceability Matrix (RTM): A document which helps project teams link the client's requirements to the specific deliverables which satisfy their needs. RTMs are usually represented in the form of matrices.

Risk: An uncertain event or condition that, if it occurs, can have a positive or negative effect on a project's objectives.[1]

Risk Register (also called Risk Log): The Risk Register is a critical tool which helps project teams track potential and actual project challenges. It is a key document usually created in the early stages of project planning. It is then updated and used throughout the project lifecycle.

Risk Response Planning: The process of developing strategic options and determining actions to enhance opportunities and reduce threats to the project's objectives.

Scope: Work that needs to be accomplished to deliver a product, service, or result which meets client-specified features and functions.

Scope Creep: Changes and continuous or uncontrolled growth in a project's scope, without commensurate adjustments for cost, time, and resources.

Sponsor: The individual or group providing resources and support for a project. Sponsors are accountable for the project's success. Project Sponsors are also responsible for ensuring that a project delivers the agreed business benefits.

Stakeholder: Any individual, group or organization who may affect, be affected, or have the perception of being affected by a decision, activity, or outcome of a project.

Student Syndrome: The practice of leaving a lot of unfinished work until the last moment, while originally working at a very relaxed pace.

Task: An activity that needs to be accomplished within a defined period or by a deadline to work towards work-related goals.

Waterfall: A design process often used in software development. The model is named after the cascading steps in its lifecycle: requirements, design, construction, testing, installation, and maintenance.

Work Breakdown Structure (WBS): A deliverable-oriented representation of project scope which is a handy tool for project teams to decompose work into progressively smaller parts. The WBS is considered to be the foundation of project planning.

Work Package: The smallest unit of work that a project can be broken down into when creating the WBS. Project teams use work packages as the basis for planning, assigning, and tracking activities.

CPSIA information can be obtained
at www.ICGtesting.com
Printed in the USA
FSHW011959020719
59680FS

9 781947 949034